The Mirror and the Hammer

h

The Mirror and the Hammer

Challenging Orthodoxies in Psychotherapeutic Thought

Ernesto Spinelli

CONTINUUM
London and New York

Continuum
The Tower Building, 11 York Road, London SE1 7NX
370 Lexington Avenue, New York, NY 10017-6503

www.continuumbooks.com

First published 2001

British Library Cataloguing-in-Publication Data
A catalogue record for this book is available from the British Library.

ISBN 0 8264 5211 6

Typeset by CentraServe Ltd, Saffron Walden, Essex
Printed and bound in Great Britain by CPD Wales

For my friends and colleagues
in The Society for Existential Analysis

Contents

Introduction

Recently, a client of mine whom I have been seeing for a number of years asked me: 'If I ask you a straightforward question, will you give me a straightforward answer?' After our mutual laughter had ceased, he added: 'Please don't say something like: "It depends on what the question is." Just trust me, alright?'

I decided I could, and would. 'Ask,' I said.

'Have you begun writing another book?' he enquired.

I smiled. 'Yes,' I confessed. 'What made you guess that I was?'

He replied: 'For one thing, you're dressing even more sloppily than usual. Your hair is longer and more 'free-floating' than ever. And . . .' He paused.

'And . . .?' I encouraged.

'And your comments and questions seem a lot more challenging than usual. You're really on the ball.'

'Does this disturb you?'

'No, not at all!' he asserted. 'If anything, it makes me wish you'd write more frequently!'

'Even if I had nothing new or interesting to say?'

'What,' he wondered, 'is there that is new or interesting to say about psychotherapy?'

'That's exactly what I ask myself each time I sit down to write this new book of mine,' I grinned.

'Don't worry about it,' my client consoled me. 'Therapy just is, isn't it? It's everywhere now, in everything and everybody. Nothing makes sense if it hasn't been subjected to therapy.'

'Thank you,' I said.

After he had left, I sat and thought about this snippet of our conversation. Somehow, my mind engaged in some 'free-floating attention' that eventually settled upon the realization of how rapidly novel psychotherapy-influenced buzzwords, such as *empty nest syndrome*, are accepted into everyday discourse as the latest in an ever-growing sequence of psychic terrors most people will have to face up to and learn to live with – preferably with the assistance of a surfeit of chat shows dedicated to the problem and shelves full of 'self-help' manuals and guides written by self-proclaimed experts and gurus. I asked myself whether this syndrome, like so many others, named and expressed a long-felt, if previously 'uncaptured', parental experience or whether the disorienting and destabilizing experiences associated with the term had begun to emerge subsequent to its invention.

These contemplations brought me back to my client; not only to his statement about psychotherapy's all-pervasive influence but, more interestingly, to the awareness that his very method of inference and enquiry was expressive of a psychotherapeutically informed methodology. At that point, I decided he had been correct in his assertion. Then I asked myself: 'And if so, then. . .'

The topics discussed in this book focus upon some of the speculations that followed on from the above uncompleted sentence. They deal with issues and concerns that have beguiled me for a number of years and that are united by the psychotherapeutic 'lens' through which they are perceived and examined.

My primary aim in writing this text has been to provide readers with what I hope are worthwhile challenges to a number of deep-rooted and at times inflexible stances and assumptions that typically have been promulgated by psychotherapists and that have subsequently permeated public consciousness and opinion. As well as criticize, I have also made the attempt to offer reformulations that may better address the issues under examination. The book is concerned with two broad arenas of focus.

The first of these critically examines several fundamental underlying principles of contemporary psychotherapeutic thought and practice. Chapter 1 asks the disturbing question: 'What has happened to psychotherapy?' and, hopefully, provides an equally disturbing reply. Chapter 2 considers the vexing question of psychotherapists' divided stances towards and (more typically) avoidance of any form of personal disclosure during psychotherapy. Chapter 4 attempts to provide a legitimate alternative to the hypothesis of the unconscious as a separate and distinct mental system. The final chapter challenges psychotherapy's espousal of a particular type of 'professionalism' as exemplified by the kinds of relationships between practitioner and client that it promotes and upon which it relies.

The second focal point of this text explores how psychotherapeutic ideas in general, and psychoanalytic perspectives in particular, have not only permeated but also reshaped our society's ways of thinking about and understanding various seminal features and expressions of 'being human'. The chapters in this section deal with our views and assumptions regarding self (Chapter 3), sexuality (Chapter 5), the relationship between childhood and sexuality (Chapter 6), the problem of evil (Chapter 7), artistic creativity (Chapter 8), and our stance towards the uncanny and the unknown (Chapter 9). In addition, I will present and consider what may be more adequate alternatives to each of these suppositions as derived from my understanding of a number of pivotal insights provided primarily by existential phenomenology.

As is the case for so much else in my life, I am indebted to my wife, Maggi Cook, for having provided me with the title to this book. Maggi tells me that in a discussion about the power and impact of cinema upon culture, V. I. Lenin suggested the analogy of 'a mirror and a hammer'. Lenin's proposal was that film does not merely permit a reflection, or 'mirroring' of society. More than this, it opens up novel, even radical, possibilities for altering our perspectives and, thereby, acts as 'a hammer' in that it both demolishes old vistas and provides the instrument required for the creation of the new.

When I heard Maggi's account, I was immediately struck by the aptness of this analogy with regard to psychotherapy's role in and influence upon our culture. On further consideration, it also occurred to me that both cinema and psychotherapy are generally considered to have been 'born' in the same year: 1895. Without seeking to over-extend this serendipitous conjunction, nevertheless let me also add that while cinema and psychotherapy provide key defining characteristics of the twentieth century, their potential as means of liberation from stagnant ways of conceiving of, and relating to, ourselves and our world has, over the years, been significantly eroded. Instead, at least to a substantial degree, each has become a conduit for the pacification and control of the unruly stirrings of personal and social unease.

Should it achieve its intended purpose, may this book be experienced both as 'a mirror and a hammer'.

A note about the text

A number of the themes under discussion have been previously presented (albeit in different style and structure) in several talks delivered to the Society for Existential Analysis during the years when it was my great honour to serve as its Chair (1993–9).

The Society for Existential Analysis came into being in 1988 through the impetus and energy of its Founding Chair, Emmy van Deurzen. I continue to count it as one of the great blessings in my life that I was invited to attend its first meeting. Since those pioneering days, the Society has grown enormously, such that, today, as well as its having attained international recognition and respect through its journal and conferences, it also acts as an accrediting organization for existential psychotherapy training programmes within the United Kingdom Council for Psychotherapy (UKCP).

What has not changed, however, is the society's continuing aim of providing an open forum for the analysis and exchange of existential-phenomenological ideas and viewpoints and their implications for the theory and practice of psychotherapy.

Those readers who might want to find out more about the Society, or who would like to join it, should contact:

The Society for Existential Analysis
BM Existential
London WC1N 3XX
www.existential.mcmail.com

1 Celebrating mediocrity: what has happened to psychotherapy?

A year or so ago, I read the following quote by Murray Kempton:

> I cannot conceal the sense that those of my subjects who became communists were terribly flawed by their acceptance of a gospel which had no room in it for doubt, or pity, or mercy. And that clutching its standard, it was inevitable that so many would set out to become redeemers, and end up either policemen or the targets of policemen.[1]

Although Kempton was writing about the experiences of 1930s' communists in the United States, when I mentally exchanged the word 'communists' in the above passage with that of 'psychotherapists', I was immediately struck by how deeply and accurately the passage resonated for me. I began to wonder: What has happened to psychotherapy?

Of late, I find myself returning to this question more and more frequently. In one sense, the answer is somewhat obvious. Psychotherapy has developed at an astonishing rate over the past decade. The number of training programmes, academic institutes and centres dedicated to its study and analysis have multiplied significantly. In similar fashion, where once, not so long ago, public attitudes towards psychotherapy were characteristically wary, today its obvious acceptability is everywhere evident in the media, in GP medical practices and alternative health clinics, in educational establishments, in family and legal mediation services.[2]

My own professional career has revolved around teaching and practising psychotherapy, writing about it and either conducting research or assisting Master's- and Doctoral-level candidates with the development of their own research. The Institute I work at, The School of Psychotherapy and Counselling at Regent's College, has established itself as one of the largest and most prestigious psychotherapeutic training centres in Britain and has just launched its own textbook series, published by Continuum. More specifically, the therapeutic approach that I advocate, *existential psychotherapy*, continues to establish itself as a prominent, and critical, alternative to the more dominant psychoanalytic, cognitive-behavioural and humanistic schools and has begun to have significant impact upon, and within, both private and public clinics and hospital psychotherapy units.

Recognizing all of the above developments, and many more that I have not mentioned, the success of psychotherapy is all too evident. And yet . . .

A while back, I found myself taking part in a telephone phone-in on psychotherapy. I was both touched and amazed by the honesty and openness of the callers, by their willingness both to reveal their painful tales and have them reconsidered, reshaped and temporarily redressed both by myself and the ebullient radio announcer who hosted the proceedings. What amazed me even more, however, was that every single person with whom I had had any sort of contact from the moment I had stepped into the broadcast building – from the PA who had first come to greet me, to the radio announcer, to the production manager, to the anonymous audience members who spoke so candidly of their lives – all of them had expressed, directly and unhesitatingly, their full and unquestioning acceptance of psychotherapy as being 'a good and worthwhile enterprise'. And here I was, the only registered psychotherapist among them, asking myself and, eventually, everyone else tuned into the station: 'Do you really think it *is* such a good thing?' As soon as I uttered these words, the radio announcer stared at me, eyes wide open in disbelief and worry that I had gone temporarily insane, and then, laughing somewhat too brightly, announced a sudden commercial break. Needless to say, I have not been invited back to that particular radio station.

What concerns forced me to raise that question?

In its earliest years, psychotherapy was a powerful critic of dominant cultural views and assumptions. Somehow, over time, it appears to have reshaped itself (or has been reshaped) into one of the primary advocates of our current *Zeitgeist*. It reflects, as many have suggested, 'the spirit of our time'. This state of affairs reminds me of Jean-Paul Sartre's infamous – if accurate – pronouncement that every movement of liberation will eventually become one of oppression.[3]

Is this what has happened to psychotherapy? Some, myself included, might suggest that psychotherapy has succumbed to a particular form of virulent madness: the madness of dubious 'facts' and questionable conclusions masquerading as reason and rationality. It seems to me that psychotherapy, perhaps like so much else in our current culture, has learned to chant a distinctly counter-Coué mantra: 'Every day, in every way, I get worse and worse'.[4]

At present, there exist approximately 400 different forms of psychotherapy. All of them are, more or less, mad. And all of them express this madness, as the experiential psychotherapist Alvin Mahrer has recently asserted, via the language of psychobabble. Mahrer writes:

> **One of the main things that characterises psychotherapists and that distinguishes them from others is their spouting of psychobabble. They learn to say terms that give the illusion of genuine knowledge, of professionalism, of science. They are elite and specialised because they spout jargon terms like: unconditional positive regard, contingency control, transference,**

reframing, double bind, existential analysis, bioenergetics, phallic stage, archetype, multimodal therapy, systematic desensitization, cognitive schema, catharsis, impulse control, ego-diffusion. . . . Psychotherapists are distinguished mainly by their using these terms with effortless ease, as if they knew what the terms meant.

Then they can speak in impressive paragraphs such as this, taken from a table of random psychobabble phrases: 'This client is characterised by free-floating anxiety and a borderline disorder, brought about by a traumatic childhood history of emotional abuse, lack of stable support system, and an inadequate cognitive development. Accordingly, the treatment of choice is systemic therapy, with retraining of core conceptual schemata to heighten self-efficacy in a supportive therapist– client alliance, emphasising positive regard and minimizing interpretative probing into stressful pockets of serious psychopathology.' The speaker may have no idea what she is saying, or may even secretly know that she is playing the game of silly psychobabble, but if she carries it off with professional aplomb, she can probably be accepted into the inner ranks of professional psychotherapists.[5]

Mahrer's words resonate with a typically provocative declaration made by Friedrich Nietzsche: as long as you are *seen* to believe in a supposed truth with sufficient conviction and passion, others will come to believe in it as well. But more, he adds, even if it should come to a point in time when you, yourself, begin to harbour doubts about the worth and truth of these self-same beliefs, now it will be the others' faith in the beliefs, and in you as the belief-bringer, that will serve to eradicate that felt sense of doubt and re-convince you of their – and your – inherent veracity and importance.[6]

This argument, it seems to me, may well provide vital clues to how psychotherapy has been so successful and has come to achieve such a central place in our culture. Equally, however, it may well also suggest the path to psychotherapy's debasement and eventual decline.

In an earlier book, *Demystifying Therapy*, I argued that, in many cases, the theoretical assumptions that underpin psychotherapeutic practice, and the specialist terminology and language of psychotherapy, as well as serving to confound and mystify the process for both psychotherapist and client also provoke what I have somewhat facetiously termed the *Dumbo effect*.[7] For, just like Walt Disney's famous cartoon elephant who believed that he was able to fly only because he possessed a 'magic feather', psychotherapists have incorrectly placed their faith in sets of principles and assumptions that are questionable, unnecessary and, most pertinently, that may themselves be the basis for the many and varied criticisms and concerns being expressed about the profession.

For psychotherapists to begin to question and doubt the veracity of their 'magic feathers' is no easy task, not least because such an enterprise raises fundamental questions about the professional 'specialness' of psychotherapy. Yet what alternative is there for a profession that, after all, takes this very same demand to be the integral task of its clientele?

As far as can be ascertained from current research, the present status of all the existing models of psychotherapy is best characterized by their inability to demonstrate reliable and valid evidence for any specific determining factor that might explain their overall efficacy. Similarly, there exists no clearly defined basis to assert the superiority of any one model over all – or even most – others in provoking beneficial outcomes. Recently, various important texts that have summarized the major research that has studied both outcome evidence and process factors have succeeded in reconfirming the generally perceived viewpoint that no matter how absurd the model of therapy might appear to be to professionals and public alike, it cannot be demonstrated that such a model is less likely than any other to be effective in reducing psychic disturbances. More confounding, perhaps, is the persistence of tangential, if recurrent, data suggestive of the conclusion that, at least in some cases, successful outcomes are more likely to occur when the 'providers' of psychotherapeutic interventions have had no training whatsoever in the profession.[8]

None the less, while it is legitimate to conclude that we may not know just why it is likely that psychotherapeutic input will have beneficial consequences, or what the critical factors are that may increase their prospect, it would be false to conclude that psychotherapy does not 'work'. It does; and it does so most of the time.[9] It is the 'how and what' of it that continue to befuddle both practitioners and researchers. My personal conclusions regarding this current impasse have led me to question the value of our professional (over)reliance upon the *theories and models* that we espouse, apply in our practise and with which we identify our roles as psychotherapists.

Psychotherapists tend, obviously, to emphasize their own preferred models, and the years of training they have undertaken to understand and become specialists in their (often arcane) wisdom, as the specific determinants for psychotherapeutic insight and beneficial outcome. However, it may be the case that the import of such factors lies only with regard to the 'Dumbo effect' that they provoke. In other words, these specific factors, by means of a circular logic all too frequent in psychotherapeutic theories, provide the basis for psychotherapists' continuing *belief* in the efficacy and superiority of a specific model, and, as well, allow advocates of competing models to distinguish and contrast what they do with what other psychotherapists do. However, on the basis of existing research, it may be the case that these factors are important only insofar as they serve to sustain psychotherapists' *beliefs in* their expertise (or 'magic') and provide them with a *rationale* for their interventions. Further, as Nietzsche's injunction reminds us, such beliefs are likely to be shared and invested with power by the psychotherapists' clients who, in turn, maintain and, if necessary, rekindle their psychotherapists' waning and wavering of trust in the model's worth and efficacy through their own beliefs in the beneficial impact of the model-driven psychotherapeutic interventions upon their lives.

If, rather than dismiss this anxiety-provoking challenge, psychotherapists were more willing to examine their assumptions, then one possibility that emerges is that there may be very little in psychotherapy that is *not* a 'Dumbo effect'. Ah . . . But does not the possibility of such a conclusion serve to add to the sense of unease surrounding psychotherapy rather than reduce or resolve it? Sadly, yes.

A great deal of my concern regarding psychotherapy rests upon the underlying assumption, accepted by the vast majority of individuals who have any kind of relationship with the profession, that it is to be primarily considered as a desirable and effective panacea for a multitude of psychosocial disorders and disturbances.

At first, this perspective might well appear to make a great deal of sense. After all, why should anyone subject him or herself to psychotherapeutic interventions, or, indeed, why should anyone invest so much time, emotional and intellectual effort and income both to train and practise as a psychotherapist, if there were not some underlying premise that this might provide at least the possibility of obtaining or providing beneficial outcomes?

While it would be both false and absurd for me to deny that beneficial outcomes usually emerge from psychotherapeutic interventions, none the less I want to propose an alternative focus for psychotherapy. It is a focus that acknowledges the likelihood of sometimes significant, sometimes subtle, ameliorative outcomes but which does not seek to make such outcomes its primary aim or goal. What, then, might be this 'new' psychotherapy's intended purpose and value?

When contrasting this alternative with the more commonly

accepted one, an implicit set of cultural assumptions around which most psychotherapy converges reveal themselves. These beliefs regarding our 'psychic well-being' may be summarized as follows:

1 All of us have the capacity, or at least the potential, to live satisfactory, worry-free lives.
2 Whatever psychic problems, worries or concerns might arise, there exist fairly straightforward means to either minimize their impact upon us or, better still, to resolve them.
3 The achievement of both of the above requires the intervention and assistance of an expert who is skilled both in the knowledge and application of 'healing techniques'.

The kindest thing that can be said of all three of these assumptions is that they are undeniably naive. As I have already argued with regard to the third assumption, it is more truthful to say that psychotherapeutic 'experts' do not really have a clue as to what aspects – if any – of their knowledge are valid and worthwhile; nor can they point to any particular skills that have either been demonstrated to be effective (such as, for instance, various forms of interpretation or transformation of meaning) or that require specialist expertise and extensive training in order to be properly applied.

As to the first two assumptions, it is evident that, as many sociopolitical, feminist and cultural critics have already argued, the different sets of conditions into which we are born will certainly 'stack the deck' in favour, or against the fulfilment of whatever potential might be there for any one of us.[10]

Just as important, I would suggest, is the realization that many – if not most – of our life problems are not easily resolvable nor, indeed, resolvable at all. For instance, one of my clients was a 68-year-old woman whose husband had recently died. Her 'problem' was that of grief and loneliness – neither of which could truly be assuaged either in the short or

long term. Some weeks after she had begun to see me, her cat
– the one other living being in her life with whom she engaged
in an ongoing, day-to-day caring and physical relationship –
died of old age. Two months later, her only sister, whom she
rarely saw but who was at least a living link to her sense of
family and personal history, also died. How is psychotherapeutic problem-solving going to deal with this client's experience
of her life and its potential for fulfilment?

I suggest that the many far from unusual circumstances like
the one above to which psychotherapy attempts to respond
make it all too evident that its primary enterprise cannot be
directed towards the attainment of a worry-free life infused
with certainty, security, and whatever other final and fixed
stance towards existence about which one might fantasize.
Rather, psychotherapy, if anything, exposes many of the vicis-
situdes of existence, revealing them to be fundamentally
unavoidable and uncontrollable, no matter how much we
might seek to protect ourselves against their impact upon our
lives.

The problems with which psychotherapy principally concerns itself are *interrelational problems*. They are problems
dealing with issues of belief and meaning and existence that
arise from the kinds of relations between our sense of our own
being and identity and our experience of other beings, or the
world in general, and who and how they will encourage,
permit or disallow us to be. As well, such problems challenge
who and how we will encourage, permit and disallow others
(or the world) to be. These are problems that cannot be 'solved'
in any fixed or definitive sense, nor can there truly exist any
'experts' who can set about resolving them on our behalf. More
to the point, these problems are not even our own, in any
exclusively personal sense, in that they are not derived from
some internal or intrapsychic set of conditions but, rather,
exist at the nexus, or meeting point, between each person and
the world of others which he or she inhabits. *The dilemmas*

that face psychotherapists and their clients cannot truly be resolved. They can only be lived.

If psychotherapists were willing to consider the possibilities of this alternative perspective, one of their first tasks would be the abdication of what is probably their most basic assumption: that they can direct the means by which another (their client) is to be helped. As I see it, if a person has the calling to help another, then that person is selling him or herself – and the world – somewhat short by seeking to become a psychotherapist.

I am well aware that the above statement may initially seem absurd to most readers. More, it may well suggest that, viewed in this way, psychotherapy becomes a somewhat pointless enterprise and occupation. Perhaps it is; but, if so, it is worthwhile asking: and what is inherently problematic about that? Viewed from a wide variety of perspectives one could rightly conclude that life itself is a pointless enterprise. That still would not preclude either its value or, for want of a better word, its beauty.

Let me attempt an alternate, if more prosaic, response. Rather than focus upon notions of usefulness and problem-solving, it might make more sense for psychotherapists to acknowledge that uncertainty and insecurity are 'parts of the package' of living and, as such, that the psychotherapeutic encounter is but one means of exploring the experiential options people may have (which, admittedly, may be very few indeed in many instances) not only so that they may find some means to live with the uncertainties and unknowns with which we are all confronted, but also that these *givens* of life may be experienced as exhilarating and joyous as well as frightening and painful.

Then what? Here, some key insights from existential psychotherapy provide at least the beginning of an answer.

As I understand and attempt to practise it, existential psychotherapy explores the lived world of the client from a perspective that considers the issues and dilemmas being presented as expressions of the client's ongoing interpersonal relations. These relations principally include the client's experience of self and others as manifested by his or her implicit assumptions, beliefs and values that contextualize a particular and embodied 'way of being'. In doing so, existential psychotherapy attempts to expose (but not divide or pathologize) what might be termed the various *existence tensions* that are expressed via that way of being.[11]

Existence tensions may most easily be understood from the standpoint of various universal polarities such as self/other, isolation/belonging, mental/physical, active/passive, good/bad, rational/emotional, freedom/determinism, and material/spiritual. Each of us constructs a stance towards living in general that expresses our position along the continuum of each of these polarities. In turn, where we locate ourselves with regard to each polarity serves both to alleviate and provoke our existence tensions. For instance, the person who must avoid the experience of being alone will require, with increasing urgency, the company of others. As such, that person's existence tensions with regard to this polarity may be expressed in terms of fears or phobias regarding any circumstances that might provoke isolation, or of experiencing near-suicidal tensions when he or she has lost or cannot find a partner, or a variety of social problems regarding that person's inability to allow his or her partner, children or friends some form of independent life experience. On the other hand, the person who feels safest or 'most real' when left alone or free from the impact and influence of others may experience existence tensions such as the fear or phobia of being in public places and participating in social activities, or of experiencing numbness or significant unease, or even revulsion when in physical or sexual contact with another, or may express the view that he or she must be somehow inadequate or 'less than human' because there exists no felt sense of affection towards others, even one's family and friends. Furthermore, in all of these situations, the person may express an overall sense of guilt, anxiety and hatred towards either self or others or both.

Significantly, what existential psychotherapy does *not* attempt is to seek to direct some means of balancing, integrating, improving or changing the lived experience of these tensions by, for instance, making the client more (or less) rational or emotional or 'real' since it views existence tensions as expressions of *the whole* of a person's way of being rather than as isolated and troublesome symptoms that can be manipulated or altered with little awareness of or regard for their contextual implications. As problematic as they can be, these tensions may well remain necessary for the maintenance of the overall stability and security (no matter how limited and limiting such may be) that the person has constructed in order to relate with and respond to the existential possibilities and demands of the world. As such, it may be the case that the seemingly ameliorative psychotherapeutic interventions whose aim is that of removing or reducing these symptomatic tensions may well, instead, provoke far greater levels of felt disturbance and anxiety in the client. My own work with clients who have been defined, or who have defined themselves, as substance abusers or addicts of one type or another, for instance, has convinced me that any insistence upon the reduction or cessation of the addictive behaviour at the start of psychotherapy, before the contextual significance of this behaviour to the whole of the client's lived way of being has been sufficiently understood, will likely provoke far less manageable levels of debilitating anxiety since that degree of security (however restrictive and harmful) which the problematic 'addiction' served to maintain is now no longer available to the client.

Instead, the existential psychotherapist seeks to gain an increasingly adequate (if always incomplete) entry into the currently lived world of the client so that this way of being may be more accurately and honestly revealed or disclosed *as it is being lived*. Fundamentally, then, the aim of the enterprise steers both psychotherapist and client towards a stance of acceptance of what it is like and how it feels to be the client who is in relationship with the psychotherapist. This acceptance is neither about approval nor disapproval of this way of being; it is, primarily, a descriptive and revelatory enterprise.

It can also be, and often is, an intensely felt and powerful challenge for the client who, in all likelihood, has rarely, if ever, been in the presence of another who does not, either implicitly or explicitly, demand that he or she be different, or change, in some way or other. This experience of another who at least attempts to accept 'the being who is present' is, in turn, likely to permit some movement towards the client's own acceptance of being whether from the perspective of 'self' or of 'other' or, most significantly, of both. In turn, this stance towards 'what is' can illuminate both how this way of being is expressed and maintained through various existence tensions so that the client can reflect upon and truly choose this way of being or, alternatively, may begin to initiate his or her own steps towards the re-evaluation of, and potential for, changing his or her overall way of being.

This 'illumination' of how the client has structured his or her interrelational possibilities may expose unnecessary or counter-productive limitations, or may, as well, reveal novel and possible alternative ways to be. Or, it may highlight the reality that the problems and conflicts which are so disturbing also serve as necessary and unalterable factors in the maintenance of a more generalized stance towards being that the client does not wish to reconsider or alter and, as such, that the one 'solution' available lies in the acknowledgement and sustenance of these limitations from a standpoint of choice. Put simply, an experiential abyss exists between the statements 'I must' and 'I choose'. If we embrace this view of psychotherapy, we are thrown into a professional enterprise far removed from that of straightforward problem-solving, goal orientation or measurement of efficacy.

What of the 'expertise' of existential psychotherapists? What sort of aptitude is required of them? Nothing quite so simple or obvious as the application of easily distinguishable and communicable 'skills'. Rather, what 'skills' there may be rely far more on qualitative elements centred around questions of 'being' rather than the more straightforwardly quantifiable and directive input derived from the 'doing' skills one might be taught and, in turn, teach to another. Such 'existential skills' (or 'being qualities') also emphasize the existential psychotherapist's own particular 'ways of being' towards the client. And, just as pertinently, they require the psychotherapist to continually attempt to remain open to, and embracing of, such challenges as uncertainty, insecurity and receptiveness towards the unforeseen possibilities of a human (and humane) engagement with another. The abdication of the security that comes with assumptions such as 'doing it right', or directing change, or of 'the expert's' superiority of knowledge and status, can therefore be understood not as some perverse belittlement or rejection of a more typical therapeutic enterprise but, rather, as necessary constituents of the primary focus and aim of existential psychotherapy. If such 'skills' provoke deep unease for the psychotherapist, is it not also the case that they reflect more accurately, in their immediacy, the very same 'existence tensions' that the client seeks to convey and resolve?

How does this sort of therapy 'work'? I don't know. What is its point and purpose? I don't know. What is supposed to happen when it is applied? I don't know. Is it worthwhile? If I trust my own experience and (through their statements) that of both clients and psychotherapists who have found the courage to attempt such engagements, then yes, undoubtedly. And is this the answer, the solution, to my own and many others' concerns about psychotherapy? No. Or, to be more optimistic, not just yet.

The basis for this last conclusion rests upon numerous remaining qualms and concerns that continue to worry me (and, undoubtedly, various other existential psychotherapists) and impact upon my practice. But one, in particular, stands out for me and deserves some explication. As I will seek to demonstrate, it is a 'tension' that I believe arises from existential psychotherapy's own unwillingness or inability to consider crucial implications derived from its very advocacy of, and reliance upon, the self-same interpersonal assumptions that remain its most fundamental and substantial contribution to psychotherapeutic thought and practice.

Existential psychotherapy initially appears to many psychotherapists and clients alike as a highly attractive system. People tend to like and approve of a philosophy, and of a psychotherapeutic approach, that promotes notions of freedom, choice and responsibility – so long as these terms are understood and interpreted from a *subjective* perspective which both internalizes and isolates such notions and the actions associated with them. In other words, to be somewhat simplistic about it, if I choose to act in a way that I believe will 'free up my possibilities', but which you experience as oppressive, painful or undesirable, then from an isolationist subjective standpoint I can respond to your experience as being 'your choice' (just as my experience is of 'my' choice and making) and can abdicate any sort of responsibility for it.

This subjective perspective is evident in a wide variety of psychotherapeutic approaches (most prominently among those that fall under the broad labels of 'humanistic' and 'cognitive-behavioural'), and, as well, became a prominent feature of various self-oriented awareness and actualization training programmes such as *est*.[12] Further, this same perspective can be seen to underpin the vast majority of the more recent and increasingly fashionable 'change management' and 'personal coaching' training programmes and seminars now available to company executives. More relevantly, perhaps, this subjective misinterpretation of existential ideas remains noticeable in the work and writings of numerous psychotherapists who label themselves as 'existential'.

What is common throughout all of these subjectively focused distortions is that the more complex and disquieting implications arising from an interrelational perspective on choice, freedom and responsibility are not given their necessary exposure and consideration. *Viewed from an existential standpoint, questions of choice, freedom and responsibility cannot be isolated or contained within some separate being (such as 'self' or 'other').* In the inescapable interrelationship that exists between 'a being' and 'the world', each impacts upon and implicates the other, each is defined through the other and, indeed, each 'is' through the existence of the other. Viewed in this way, no choice can be mine or yours alone, no experienced impact of choice can be separated in terms of 'my responsibility' versus 'your responsibility', no sense of personal freedom can truly avoid its interpersonal dimensions.

Let us consider a not uncommon psychotherapeutic scenario: a man in his early forties comes to psychotherapy in order to sort out various interrelated crises in his life: his fifteen-year-long marriage has become unexciting and predictable, he is bored with his work, and wonders how he could have compromised his youthful dreams and aspirations to the point at which he now finds himself, and he has met another woman who makes him feel more alive, alert and sexual than he has felt for a great many years, and who infuses his life with newly regained meaning and possibilities. He confesses that he dearly loves his wife and two children, and does not wish to hurt any of them, but has he not the right to actualize himself and his possibilities?

Now, let us say that the psychotherapist adopts an approach

to psychotherapy which follows all of the alternatives I have suggested. The psychotherapist accepts, clarifies and challenges the way of being of the client without attempting to directly change (or judge) that way of being. Until, eventually, the client announces that, through the psychotherapy, he is now absolutely clear that what he wants is his new life, that he is prepared to be honest with his wife and children, friends and co-workers, and that, while anxious, he is prepared to face the uncertainties that will come with his starting a new life, giving up his job, and so forth.

From a *subjective* perspective, the psychotherapeutic work is done: the client is 'more real and honest', more focused in his intentions, more integrated. From an *interrelational* perspective, however, there remains a great deal for the client to consider and confront. What does he imagine the effect that his decision will have upon his relations with his wife, his children, his friends, his co-workers? What does he imagine their experience of his decision to be? What does he imagine the impact of his decision upon the relationship between his wife and each of the children? Or between the children? Or between any of them and his friends? Or his colleagues and co-workers?

In other words, there exist so many interrelational realms upon which his decision impacts that it would be intersubjectively irresponsible not to attend to at least those which the client himself takes to be meaningful and relevant. These explorations are not intended to influence the client's decision, nor to instil some sort of intersubjective morality upon him, nor to bring the actual views of all these others in the client's world to his consideration. Rather, this emphasis upon these more *world-focused dimensions* serves to implicate his decision, his newly chosen way of being, in such a way that it includes his lived experience of the world, and the others who exist within it, as it is in all its confounding complexity, rather than permit him to avoid its consideration or to construe and maintain the possibility of a world that does not fit his lived experience.

Sadly, I suspect that most psychotherapists, including existential psychotherapists, will balk at my insistence that these world dimensions be made so explicit. They will, in all likelihood, argue that to do so may well threaten, either in part or as a whole, the relationship that has been built up between themselves and their clients. But I cannot see how one can promote an interpersonal perspective and avoid these considerations. For too long, 'the world' – other than via its being represented by the psychotherapist – has been left out of (if not evicted from) the consulting room. This might be understandable from the viewpoint of other psychotherapeutic models whose focus remains upon the intrapsychic and the subjective, but it cannot be so for the existential model.

This concern, in turn, provokes (for me, at least) various other areas of unease that can be extrapolated from the above analysis (not least among them those concerns around existential psychotherapists' attempts to preserve their anonymity and to avoid personal disclosure – the topic taken up in Chapter 2). None the less, if this issue can be more carefully and honestly taken up by existential psychotherapists, its impact will extend in some fashion to all models and approaches.

I began this chapter with the question: What has happened to psychotherapy? In one sense, an answer that might be given to such a question is: Not much at all. Psychotherapy has largely remained within the trajectory set for it just over a hundred years ago. It continues to wrestle with the very same problems presented to it by its advocates and critics. It is as perplexing, invigorating and irritating as ever. All that has changed is that it has increasingly tended to become an ally of dominant cultural assumptions rather than one of culture's most trenchant critics. In so doing, it has puffed itself up in its pomposity and uncritical sense of its own self-importance. As a result, it seems to me that psychotherapy has encased itself within a set of restrictive interventions that doom its enterprise to a stagnant mediocrity which cannot be surpassed so long as it insists upon keeping the world out of the consulting room. Worse than this, however, in adopting this isolationist perspective, psychotherapy, however inadvertently, has blunted its socially critical edge to such a degree that, currently, its major achievements are those that celebrate its growing acceptance of, and by, the status quo. In this sense, then, the once revolutionary possibilities of psychotherapy have given way to nothing more or less than the celebration of a self-serving mediocrity. I have attempted to counter this by suggesting some possible alternatives which, in turn, have provoked a different, if related, question: What future lies in store for psychotherapy?

Again, at my most objective, I would conclude that, if it maintains its current focus, aims and identity, psychotherapy will quickly go the way of many outmoded and redundant twentieth-century artefacts and be subsumed by more focused, short-term and goal-specific psychobiological interventionist programmes – as has already begun to become evident in North America. However, in those moments when I find myself experiencing or 'living' psychotherapy as a practitioner, a teacher of sorts and a theoretician, I both regret and rebel against this likelihood. Instead, I conceptualize, and seek to put into practice, various stances and possibilities that attempt to disturb the dominant path and shake psychotherapy out of the hermetically sealed and arcane confines of the 'special and exclusive' relationship between client and psychotherapist which maintains and elevates the rampant subjectively focused, 'intrapsychic imperialism' so favoured by our culture. This 'elevation of the self' made psychotherapy into an attractive enterprise. It has also begun to reveal itself as its agent of undoing.

The alternatives I have suggested place psychotherapy within a much more uncertain and anxiety-provoking territory wherein its purpose and function is not so immediately clear-cut, its potential requires novel means of analysis and meas-urement, its focus shifts from subjectively focused problem-solving to intersubjective explorations of the implica-tions and possibilities of a given way of being, and in which the role and expertise of the psychotherapist shifts from that of helper, healer and instructor back to its original meaning of 'attendant' – one who walks beside you and, through being with you, illuminates not just your world, but all worlds as well. These alternatives re-inject a significant measure of social awareness and criticism in psychotherapeutic thought and practice. They may make enemies of its current benefactors and, even if adopted, they may still prove to lead to failure.

The choice is stark. And starker still is the possibility that it may already have been made.

2 To disclose or to not disclose – that is the question

Imagine, for a moment, that your professional expertise lies in the arena of consultancy. You maintain a private office which is suitably equipped for your professional consultations with your clients whom you meet at prearranged and specified dates and times. What might most concern you about the appearance of this private space? Would you, for instance, seek to ensure that it exuded an air of neutrality or even anonymity such that nothing whatsoever within it would reveal any aspect of your personality, your interests, your professional and private life? For example, would you avoid the presence of any books that might divulge your taste and interests in reading material? Would you ensure that whatever pictures or paintings that hung on its walls meant nothing to you at all, were as neutral as the chairs upon which you and your clients will sit? Would you ponder what possible meaning and reaction might be provoked in your clients by the discernible presence (or absence) of a box of tissues, a business diary, or family photographs?

In your professional dealings with the clients who come to see you, would you consider all the possible implications and permutations of meaning that might arise should you shake hands with them upon their arrival or exit? Would you worry about what to do or say should you happen to meet your clients in other settings – while walking down your local high street, or queuing for cinema tickets, or attending a gathering organized by a mutual acquaintance? And if, while in your office, your client might accidentally drop a personal belonging – say a pen, a hat, a pair of gloves – and appear to remain unaware of this, would it provoke all manner of concerns and considerations as to what, if anything, might be appropriate behaviour on your part?

And if, in the course of your discussions with your client, you were to find yourself being asked as to whether you had visited such and such a place, or read a particular text, or, more daringly, whether you are married or have a family, would you already have acquired sufficient skills with which to deflect such queries, or turn them back upon your inquisitor in such ways that they would require an explanation as to what meaning and significance these matters might hold for him or her?

All these, and a great many more possible scenarios, and the gravity of deliberation that each provokes, infuse the tribulations of a great many psychotherapists. They are perceived as quandaries requiring minute analysis and attention with regard to their intent and how to go about dealing with them both by the troubled psychotherapist and his or her clinical supervisor.

And if, as is likely, the reader is provoked into gales of bemused laughter by the absurd seriousness with which such matters are treated, beware the consequent psychotherapeutic response: 'You have failed to understand the special nature of the relationships that psychotherapists foster. Your reaction betrays your naivety regarding the subtle strategies that make up the psychotherapist's expertise.'

But, please, do continue to laugh; although I label myself a psychotherapist, I find that, with increasing frequency, I laugh along with you. All the above concerns fall into the broad psychotherapeutic category known as *disclosure*. More accurately, the issues focus upon *psychotherapists'* disclosures since it is both assumed and expected that clients will disclose a great deal of their life experience to their psychotherapist.

The origins of these near-mystical concerns can be discerned, like so much else in psychotherapy, in the early treatises regarding the proper and approved practice of psychoanalysis. Some of these injunctions come to us from Sigmund Freud himself, although it must be said that he at least tended to suggest that these were not so much iron-clad rules but, rather, more akin to points of consideration. In any case, it is evident that, in his own practice, Freud was consistent in either breaking or paying little heed to these decrees.[1]

The desire at the heart of the issue of disclosure is that of the psychotherapist's maintenance of his or her *anonymity*. It is argued that, in remaining anonymous, the psychotherapist can become a sort of 'blank screen' upon which clients can project all their fears, wishes, guilt, love and aggression. It follows, if one accepts this argument, that the intrusion of the psychotherapist's own disclosed material will confuse these projections and make the psychotherapeutic enterprise more complex and confounding than it already is.[2] In addition, some theories have also argued that the effect of such disclosures may be seen by the client to be some sort of defensive assertion of psychic power and authority on the part of the psychotherapist and that clients will, albeit unconsciously, respond to these as instances of an abusive attitude towards them.[3]

Although most of the more strident objections towards psychotherapist disclosures have eased somewhat over time, and, consequently, have been the subject of critique and reformulation, many of these attitudes and regulations remain fixed in some form or other for the vast majority of psychotherapists – regardless of the model they espouse. While there exists a range of perspectives that might be categorized as extending from the 'fundamentalist' to the 'liberal', anything more revolutionary (in either direction) has been effectively shut out from currently approved discourse. Even existential psychotherapists who have consistently criticized and rejected most of the theoretical assumptions of psychoanalysis in particular and of many subsequent psychotherapies in general, have, on the whole, retained and advanced most of these same concerns with little hesitation or question.

On the other hand, and perhaps most famously, those psychotherapists who practise from humanistic perspectives have tended to reject most vehemently the strictures upon their relationships with clients imposed by the decree against psychotherapist disclosure. They have argued that these limitations prevent them from being 'real' with their clients and that, in turn, this unreality encroaches upon the possibility of an open and honest engagement.[4]

While I sympathize with these concerns and accept their general validity within the theoretical framework of humanistic psychotherapy, I would argue that this perspective addresses only one side of the complexity of issues surrounding the question of disclosure. My own experiences with humanistic psychotherapists alerted me to this.

As an undergraduate in Canada, I participated and trained in a number of humanistic (principally person-centred) approaches, but, by 1974, I had grown disillusioned with their promise. I had glimpsed what even then I had begun to suspect to be issues of misuse of psychotherapeutic authority and power – both as possibility and experiential 'fact'. I had witnessed firsthand, for example, how the claims to 'being real or open' with clients had allowed a fair number of humanistic psychotherapists to direct and impose their views and assumptions upon them and, quite frankly, I had become disgusted – even, dare I say, 'nauseated' – by the flagrant assertion of self-elevating and other-invalidating power that humanistic therapists had permitted themselves. Even worse, I noted how I, too, had fallen into this trap and, to this day, I carry the burden of shame for things which in my unmitigated arrogance I said and did to my early clients. Having resolved to cease such, I turned away from humanistic models and embraced what I then thought to be 'the one, true model of therapy' – psychoanalysis – which I believed had seen through such abuses via its insistence upon the maintenance of the psychotherapist's neutrality and anonymity. This 'confession' should give readers some idea of how naive I was!

My initial (and uncompleted) training as a psychoanalyst revealed to me that analysts, too, were not always strict adherents of their own rules of disclosure. For instance, not long after I had joined an analytic therapy group, I was dumbfounded to witness the flagrant disclosure of significant personal material by one of my analysts. My first thought upon hearing her revelations was: 'But this is completely unprofessional! How can this woman call herself a psychoanalyst and at the same time permit herself to tell me these intimate details of her life?' However, on reflection, a second consideration arose: 'No matter how contrary to the theory to which we both subscribe this might be, is it not also gloriously affirmative of our shared humanity?' For a moment, the analyst had allowed herself to engage with me in a manner that had openly revealed an aspect of her life that invited some degree of unfettered contact, some form of human warmth and engagement. Both of those examples from my varied training encapsulate for me the dilemmas with which the issue of psychotherapists' disclosures presents.

Humanistic psychotherapists, believing in the value of self-disclosure, fail to address the issue that such disclosures are not 'across the board'. Rather, they choose when and how and what to disclose to their clients about their lives, but the basis for this decision is rarely formulated or considered. Indeed, my suspicion is that were they to carry out analyses concerning 'the when and what and how' of their disclosures, humanistic psychotherapists might well be shocked by what such analyses revealed. I would not be too surprised if these raised important questions regarding humanistic psychotherapists' assumptions about 'openness', 'transparency' and 'congruity' and, instead, confronted them with their defensiveness, their authoritarianism, and their desire both to elevate themselves and to be elevated in the eyes of their clients.

On the other hand, the psychoanalytic stance advocating absolute non-disclosure is equally open to question on several grounds. First, no matter what environment analysts create for their consulting rooms, it will undoubtedly disclose *some* aspects of their undisclosed lives. This should be obvious to psychoanalysts who, by their own credo, have taught us that one discloses as much by what one chooses not to state as by what one does state. No statement, be it verbal, behavioural or environmental, is truly neutral – not even a statement focused upon the maintenance of neutrality. However, much more to the point, in their silences, their 'body language', their comments upon or interpretations of their clients' discourse, psychoanalysts cannot help but disclose various personal views, issues and attitudes of their own. When contrasted with the reality of therapeutic encounters, the psychoanalytic stance towards non-disclosure reveals itself to be a fantastic self-deception. Equally, one must ask: what are the effects upon clients when they discover – as they undoubtedly will – the ambivalent and contradictory messages that their analysts convey to them? Once again, I would predict that if psychoanalysts were willing to examine those occasions in which, however inadvertently, they broke their 'rule of non-disclosure', they, too, might well discover all too similar variables to those previously mentioned with regard to humanistic psychotherapists' disclosures.

What, then, is it about the issues raised by therapeutic disclosures that so many psychotherapists treat them with such reverence? In part, I would suggest, as I have argued in Chapter 1, that these stances and concerns can be seen to make up important aspects of the 'Dumbo effect' required by psychotherapists so that they can both initiate and maintain the core beliefs that provide meaning to their notion of 'doing psychotherapy'. In similar fashion, these variables may well make up

important elements of the ritual and ceremony of psychotherapy as understood by clients. That is to say, they serve as
'superstitious principles' which, while bereft of any evidence
in favour of their import and validity, are none the less
bequeathed with a significance that is all too similar to that
accredited to articles of religious faith.

No matter how absurd these magical belief systems might
appear to some, psychotherapists continue to argue that they
remain essential aspects of the 'special and unique' relationship they attempt to engender with their clients. Further, they
insist, such issues also serve to maintain and reinforce responsible professional parameters of practice designed, principally,
to protect the client from any number of potentially calamitous
consequences arising out of unbounded emotions likely to be
experienced – and acted upon – by psychotherapist and client
alike. These concerns surrounding 'unruly affects' not only
point to various recurring concerns about coercion and abuse
– be it physical, emotional, sexual or financial – but also focus
psychotherapists upon the possible consequences that might
arise when the neglect or abdication of these concerns provokes a blurring and confounding of boundaries within a
professional relationship.

While I agree that these last points in particular are of
critical significance to psychotherapists of any persuasion, and
that they require due diligence and responsibility, I am not as
convinced as other colleagues that the options available are
quite so clear-cut as those outlined above. I will return to this
point in the final chapter.

For now, let me concede that the controversy surrounding
disclosure, while fabricating a certain degree of mystificatory
speciousness, might also serve both to define and protect the
psychotherapeutic relationship. But is the psychoanalytic
strategy that has been adopted and adapted by so many psychotherapists necessarily the *only* option open to those who
wish to avoid the consequences of breakdowns in the psycho-

therapeutic relationship as might be instigated either by the neglect or abuse of psychotherapists' disclosures?

I think that, if they were to look, existential psychotherapists might well discern a worthwhile alternative. I do not pretend to have resolved this question but, in the spirit of disclosure, let me offer my current views for readers to assess their worth. I will begin with two brief examples from my own practice.

Some time ago, I was seeing a client, Jane, who had initially come to me deeply troubled by her experiences of insecurity in various aspects of her life – particularly with regard to her role as 'a mother'. Some eight months into our sessions, she announced that she was now ready to reveal something that greatly concerned and disturbed her and which, she felt, might destroy our relationship in that, once revealed, the information might well lead me to label her as 'crazy'. She began to speak of her daughter who had been diagnosed as autistic by various experts. Jane told me that, in spite of this diagnosis, she and her husband had decided to pursue the project of educating their daughter, initially by teaching her to read and write. They had devised a number of educative games that had stimulated their daughter's interest and had succeeded in being conducive to her social and intellectual development.

At some point during these games, Jane had noticed that her daughter displayed an uncanny ability in predictively out-guessing various aspects of the game in question. For instance, when Jane and her daughter began to play the game of 'adding numbers', she had been flabbergasted to discover that her daughter would begin to write down the correct numbers to be added, and their result, *before* Jane had told her what they were. Indeed, Jane had ascertained that she would begin her writing *at the very instant in which Jane thought of the numbers*. Being a scientist by profession, and, as well, being deeply sceptical of any claims regarding so-called 'paranormal' abilities, Jane began to experiment in order to ensure that her daughter's successes were not due to some subtle, sensory-derived cues that she might be inadvertently providing.

So Jane and her daughter began to play such 'guessing games', initially in separate parts of their house and, subsequently, from different buildings. In all cases, Jane's daughter continued to achieve successful 'guesses' at astronomical degrees of statistical significance. During succeeding months, Jane's daughter's abilities extended beyond the specified 'game times' and manifested themselves in all manner of ways. It became common, for example, for either Jane or her husband to return home with the ingredients for the night's meal only to find that their daughter had already laid out the various cooking utensils, herbs and spices and so forth required for the meal's preparation. There is more – far more – that Jane told me, but such details are not essential for the purposes of this discussion.

When Jane completed her account, I noted her hesitancy in looking at me. She was embarrassed to have revealed her tale and anxious as to my reaction both to its content and my assessment of it – and, more pertinently, of her.

'I know that you must be thinking that I'm absolutely bonkers . . .' she began. 'No, I don't think that at all,' I interrupted her. 'In fact, I'm amazed – and for reasons which I suspect you, too, will find surprising.' Jane's facial expression changed from one of anxiety to that of open curiosity. 'Of all the possible therapists in London that you could have elected to come to,' I explained, 'you seem to have chosen not only one who is prepared to believe your story at face value, but also, almost certainly the only one who has studied such phenomena in a large number of children under experimental conditions and who has presented evidence that is in line with your own experience.'

Now it was Jane's turn to be amazed. She wept openly and

copiously in relief. 'You have no idea how desperately I've wanted to tell you and how terrified I was that you'd dismiss or reinterpret what I had to say,' she admitted.

The incident and account of her daughter's abilities, in itself, quickly lost its significance in our subsequent discussions. Its value, instead, was that it became a concrete means for Jane and I to explore her general insecurities and anxieties with regard to her identification of herself as a mother, and, thankfully, it provided the means for us to examine her wider sense of her identity through the therapeutic encounter.

My second example is as follows: James was a television producer who had come to me in order to deal with his inability to maintain a lasting and meaningful romantic relationship. Over the months that had already passed us by, he had delineated a number of brief, and ultimately painful, 'flings' he had had with several women, all of whom had been actresses. On this occasion he began to speak of his current affair with Claudia, a highly attractive young woman 'with great star potential' who was about to start filming a two-hour drama that James was directing as well as producing.

James assumed (wrongly, as it happens) that I had little knowledge of the various steps required in film production and had, at great length, provided me with 'an idiot's guide' to the intricacies of lighting, sound production, narrative effects and so on. He then began to recount a scene that he had begun to direct in which the love-making taking place between Claudia and her television lover was interspersed with brief 'shots' of her, by herself, either preparing for or cleaning up after this sexual encounter. James was very proud of this combination of film images since they would not only allow him to 'play with time' in a forcefully visual manner but would also reveal various aspects of Claudia's fictional personality in purely visual terms rather than rely upon more long-winded and artificial verbal disclosures that would break the narrative drive of the programme as a whole.

I do not know whether James was attempting to impress me or was genuinely naive about (even relatively recent) film history, but his claim to have created this visual plastification of time was patently false. I knew full well that a scene all too similar to the one being trumpeted by James had been achieved in a far more complex and subtle fashion by one of my favourite film directors, Nic Roeg, in his film *Don't Look Now.*[5]

As well as having experienced some degree of boredom by James' long-winded technical explanations, I had also found myself becoming more than a little irritated by his claim to visual narrative originality. I had a strong desire to deflate his self-aggrandizing pronouncements by disclosing to him that, as a young man, I had been so involved with and infatuated by cinema that I had seriously considered the possibility of taking up film-making as a career. Happily (and, I believe, responsibly) I chose not to disclose these personal details of my life. Instead, I made the attempt to maintain my focus upon James' way of being with me and challenged him to consider, among other things, what relation, if any, lay between the content and structure of the visual narrative he had 'invented' for Claudia's film character and his own sense of the content and structure of Claudia's relationship with him as a person and a lover. This intervention proved to be cataclysmic for James and became for him one of the crucial moments both in our therapeutic relationship and his understanding of the struggles and conflicts expressed through his search for a stable romantic relationship.

These two, admittedly brief, vignettes strike me as suitable avenues through which to explore the question of psychotherapists' disclosures. In the first vignette I obviously elected to disclose personal material, while in the second, the option taken by me was one of non-disclosure. What rationale did I employ in order to arrive at these disparate decisions?

The adoption of an existential approach to psychotherapy requires the psychotherapist to view the therapeutic process as one of *interpersonal encounter*. This encounter, I believe, expresses and illuminates various realms of dialogical focus of which three levels in particular seem to me to be essential arenas to be examined and clarified. These interrelational realms can be most simply described as being: '*I-focused*', '*you-focused*' and '*we-focused*' realms of encounter.[6] Each of these dialogical realms points to a particular, descriptively focused interrelational emphasis in the encounter, and each, in turn, can be opened to worthwhile investigation. Once again presented in a simple fashion, each realm can be distinguished in the following way:

1 The I-focused realm of encounter attempts to describe and clarify 'my experience of my 'self' being in any given relation'. What do I 'tell myself' about my current experience of me being in this encounter?
2 The you-focused realm of encounter attempts to describe and clarify 'my experience of the 'other' being in relation with me'. What do I 'tell myself' about my current experience of you being in this encounter?
3 The we-focused realm of encounter attempts to describe and clarify 'my experience of 'us' being in relation with one another.' What do I 'tell myself' about us in the immediacy of our encounter?

These 'being-focused' interrelational foci lie at the heart of what I seek to express when invoking the attitude and approach of existential therapy. As such, at the I-focused level, when I am being an existential psychotherapist, I experience who I am being in my relationship with my client and I am able to note and consider what I bring to the relationship. This could include my knowledge, my skills, my expertise, the personal and theory-based views, opinions and biases that I attempt to bracket, and my sense of my own being, as well as the particular focus I place upon my listening to the client.

Equally, at the you-focused realm of relation, I, as therapist, experience the client as 'the other' and note and consider what I interpret he or she brings to the relationship. This could include my understanding of the client's issues and concerns, their affective components such as those emotions, attitudes and values associated with the issues being expressed, and what is implied about the other's sense of his or her own being through these, and perhaps most significantly, the values, stances and attitude that I imagine the client holds towards and about, me while giving expression to these concerns.

At the we-focused realm of relation, I, as therapist, experience my 'self-being-in-relation-with-the-client' and note what emerges or is disclosed through the interaction *between* us. This could include my reflections, and their corresponding emotions upon what it is like for us to be with one another in this currently reflected moment, my sense of what we might be sharing at an experiential level and what may be being expressed by us in an indirect or metaphorical manner that is reflective of our current way of 'being together'.

In like fashion, the client, too, experiences these three interrelational realms, and much of the existential psychotherapist's challenges will focus upon descriptive clarification of the client's lived stance towards them.[7]

In addition, however, following on from some of the points made in Chapter 1, I would also maintain that it is of particular significance for the existential psychotherapist to consider a fourth interrelational realm that is 'they-focused'. This realm of encounter attempts to describe and clarify the client's experience of how those who make up his or her wider world of 'others' (extending beyond the other who is the psychotherapist) experience their own interrelational realms in response to the client's current way of being and, as well, to the novel ways of being that have presented themselves as possibilities to the client through psychotherapy.

Without belabouring this point, I suggest that although the

exploration of the client's experience of this fourth interrelational realm is crucial, the psychotherapist, too, may be confronted by previously unforeseen and challenging insights if he or she is willing to consider his or her current way of being with the client from the perspective of those professional and personal they-focused realms that impact upon his or her 'way of being a psychotherapist'.

The structured exploration of these various 'realms of encounter' both from the standpoint of the psychotherapist and the client is what I believe provides existential therapy with its uniqueness. Further, in their distinct emphasis upon the third realm in particular, existential psychotherapists are able to argue that, *through the focus upon this realm's directness and immediacy*, the remaining three realms are more adequately disclosed to clarificatory challenge.

With particular regard to the issue of psychotherapists' disclosures, I would argue that it is when the focus of attention is upon the third interrelational realm (the we-focused level) that the psychotherapist's disclosures may be both appropriate and beneficial to the client. For disclosure at this level would examine how the current 'microcosmic' relationship *both reveals and challenges* the client's 'macrocosmic' relations with self and other.[8]

In reconsidering the two examples presented above, it can be seen that my disclosure to Jane served to address and directly challenge her encounter experience at the level of the first, second (and, implicitly) the fourth realm – via the third realm. The disclosure stayed with, or *attended to*, the material she had forced herself to reveal – in spite of her conviction that it would result in my labelling her as 'bonkers'. In this instance at least, my disclosure addressed Jane's experience of being seen to be 'bonkers' by revealing a 'bonkers' experience of my own so that, through this disclosure, I could 'test out' not only whether I had heard Jane's concerns with adequate accuracy but also that, if so, my narrative could begin to voice those implicit or insufficiently expressed aspects of her experience of exposing herself to the judgement of another. In addition, via my disclosure, Jane was also challenged – by me and by herself – to reconsider the fixed (or sedimented) stance she had adopted towards her 'bonkers' mentality – whether as a mother who was 'bonkers', or as a mother who had given birth to a daughter who was 'bonkers' – and how such a definition impacted upon her wider self-identity.

On the other hand, if in my encounter with James I had disclosed my interest in and knowledge of film and the various disagreements and dissatisfactions I held personally about James' understanding and use of film narrative, such a disclosure would have served little purpose in our gaining significant clarification as to James' concerns with his relationship to Claudia, with lasting romantic relationships in general, or with his wider personal and professional relationships. While it remains possible that my disclosure may have proved useful and challenging to James in some unforeseen way (always a distinct, and unpredictable, possibility in psychotherapeutic encounters), it was simply unnecessary for me to have addressed it directly via personal disclosure in order that its potential significance to his explicit concerns might be opened to our exploration. Other alternatives were apparent, and these could be judged as being 'better options' insofar as they both attended to the content of his account and did not deviate the focus of the dialogue to quite different concerns (in this case, the dilemmas of film-making). My possible personal disclosure might well have provided James with important clues concerning his relationship with me at the level of the first and second realms in our encounter; its potential worth with regard to the third realm was, at best, open to substantial doubt and, at worst, might have hindered the further clarification of all the realms of encounter.

I must confess that, both personally and professionally, I maintain a fair amount of reticence in disclosing aspects of my life experience when it seems to me that such are principally for the sake of disclosure in and of itself and may be further instances of the solipsistic excesses and 'cult of personality' of our age. None the less, I would also hope that my unhesitant willingness to disclose the personal, whether in intimate, social or professional encounters when such disclosures present themselves as being the clearest and most straightforward means at my disposal to clarify the ideas, feelings or lived experiences I attempt to apprehend or convey remains apparent to those who 'meet' me, whether face-to-face or via my writings and lectures, or with whom I share personal or professional encounters. In summary, it is this more general view towards disclosure (and encounter) that both infuses and expresses my stance towards psychotherapeutic disclosures.

It remains my hope that this explication has succeeded in persuading readers that, with regard to the issue of psychotherapists' disclosures, the question is not whether psychotherapists should or should not disclose (as if it were truly possible to completely avoid such!), but, rather, that their concerns, more relevantly, should focus upon those conditions and circumstances wherein such disclosures can be the most direct and respectful approach to the clarification of their clients' overall ways of being in the world.

Considered in another fashion, I invite those readers who are also practising psychotherapists to conjure up an alternate reality where, in the early history of psychotherapy, it had been declared that the only permissible and psychotherapeutically sound way for practitioners to interpret and challenge their clients' statements is via the psychotherapist's personal disclosures. My hope is that, on reflection, having surmounted the initial sense of oddity aroused by the novelty of this injunction, psychotherapists will reveal themselves to be sufficiently open-minded to consider the absurdity of its stringent dismissal of all other dialogical possibilities between themselves and their clients as a challenge to their own fixed stances surrounding the necessity to avoid self-disclosure at all costs. I should add that the vast majority of those trainees whom I have asked to 'enter' this alternate reality and attempt to pursue its rule during training practice have reported back its unforeseen potential for meaningful and respectful dialogue.

Might it not be time for psychotherapists to reappraise their fear of disclosure? Surely, *that* is the far more pertinent question.

3 I am not a noun: the vagaries of the self

Who am I?

This question, I would suggest, remains the most fundamental among the many asked of psychotherapists by their clients. It is, as well, the seminal question asked by all of us whose reflections upon existence are structured within the parameters of Western culture and history. And, because it is a question that is bounded by the constraints and suppositions of our civilization, the manner in which we construe it reveals a number of implicit assumptions that ought to be made explicit. Among these assumptions, the most important (at least as far as psychotherapy is concerned) are the following:

1 The self is a 'thing', an entity, an essence.
2 The self is unitary, singular. Each human being is (or has) one self.
3 The self is internally or intrapsychically located. It is (somewhere) within each human being.
4 The self is, with few exceptions, intrinsically fixed in time. Permanence and consistency are characteristic features of the self. We recognize who we are through who we have been.
5 The self can be defined, and exists, in isolation. To know myself does not require a consideration of, dependence upon, the impact and influences of any other human being.
6 Distinctions can be made between the experience of the real, or true, self as opposed to the manifestation of an unreal, or false, self. The self can be 'true' or 'false' to itself in that it

can permit itself to deceive itself. The 'real' self can be lost, buried, prevented from developing its full potential and, happily, can be 'found' again – or for the first time (often via the experience of successful psychotherapy).

7 What is most important about the self is that it is the source and originator of our ability to process, and reflect upon, lived experience. The self is the initiator of consciousness.

These assumptions permeate as a whole or in part our psychological theories, our sociopolitical laws and precepts, our moral and ethical codes. They also promote our deepest and most disturbing fears.

We are both terrorized and mystified by accounts of those 'selves' who have somehow 'become unstuck', divided or multiplied in myriad ways – be they biochemical, psychological, behavioural or supernatural. Emotive terms like *brainwashing, split* – or *dissociated – personalities, multiple* or *sub-selves* and *possessed beings*, while providing little in the way of explanatory value, none the less get to the heart of those Western anxieties that are daily given substance by the odd behaviours and states of mind of those who we are told are mentally ill, criminal, the victims of pernicious cults and sects or the casualties of life experiences of such a distressing nature that they are no longer able 'to act like themselves' or 'be as they once were'. The former friends or family members of these individuals tell us that they have changed, are no longer recognizable, that their selves have been played with, manipulated, altered, submerged, lost and overwhelmed by alien entities: in differing ways, 'real selves' have been replaced by 'false selves'.

This way of understanding, and seemingly explaining, dramatic, even radical alterations in, or dissociations of, the self is equally applicable in far less extreme occurrences. Psychotherapists are commonly confronted with clients who assert that they feel themselves to be false or inauthentic, that their true self is unknown to them and that their desire is to find out who they 'really' are. Equally, whether through personal catastrophes, mental or familial breakdowns, points of crisis such as 'mid-life', or even as a result of psychotherapeutic interventions, some declare that the self who has been (and the life it has been leading) was a sham, once again a product of the unreal, the alien, the false.

What is apparent is that all these viewpoints, attitudes, demarcations and concerns regarding the self rest upon some permutation of the seven assumptions summarized above. None the less, as dominant and pervasive as these assumptions remain, they contain numerous problems and inconsistencies. The sense they make, while alluring, is open to multiple challenges not merely of logic but from experientially derived reflections upon one's own lived experience.

After over a century of social science research, the certainty and security of this prevalent perspective on the self has given way to more complex, less definitive outlooks. One crucial impetus to this reassessment has come from anthropological and ethnographic studies of major cultural variants in human conceptions of the self. Once we begin to 'loosen' our biased assumptions from the dominance of Western concepts of the self, we are presented with alternate world-views that place the self in an interactive flux whose relative (im)permanence is influenced by such factors as social standing and status, and more fluid, or present-oriented, notions of time.[1]

Most contemporary social scientists who study the self have come to consider the variant cultural viewpoints as *metaphorical* attempts to 'capture' the experience of self-awareness.[2] They have argued that when we attempt to define something that we do not (or cannot) fully grasp, we resort to metaphorical language designed to provide a (supposed) clarity to that which remains mysterious. This clarity is seemingly achieved by the transference of a given property, or set of properties, associated with one thing on to another. Not uncommonly, we say: This unknown thing is like X in that it looks like X or it serves a similar function to X or it evokes similar feelings for me, and so forth. Through this act of associative transference we bridge one thing to another, and sometimes this bridge is so effective that we can claim that the previously unknown thing cannot truly be distinguished from X – that it *is* X. So, for instance, some psychologists would claim that intelligence *is* the IQ score or that the degree of one's sadness *is* the length of time spent crying.[3]

This not untypical over-extension of properties from one thing to another, thereby uniting the various meanings of both, alerts us to the limitations of metaphor. For one thing, valuable as metaphors may be as forms of description, such descriptions as are evoked are not neutral or value-free. As well as being descriptive, metaphors are transformative. They shape (or reshape) that which we seek to grasp, and thereby allow some of its possibilities or potentials to be revealed, but these transformations will also occlude any number of unknown other possibilities and potentials. If metaphors allow us 'to see', they do so by framing the boundaries both of what is seen and how it is seen. If every metaphor provides a mirror, it also provides a hammer with which to demolish all other potential mirrors that, placed at different angles, would provoke competing or contradictory transformative metaphors.[4]

Even so, perhaps mainly through our growing willingness to look into the somewhat alien and distant mirrors of other cultures, over the past decade the implicit assumptions underlying the dominant Western notion of self have been subject to reconsideration. However, the impetus for this shift has not solely come about through the influences of alternate cultural challenges. Just as significant, I believe, has been the persuasive and radical critique originated by phenomenological insight and argument.

Phenomenologically influenced perspectives on the self begin by asserting its indissoluble and indivisible *interrela-*

tional grounding. Nothing meaningful can be stated or experienced about 'self' without an implicit reliance upon the self's interrelational placement *in the world.* My ability to state anything at all about myself requires the existence of instances of 'not-self' or, more plainly, *others* (other human beings, other living things, the world in general) in order for that statement to hold any meaning. For instance, consider some basic statements any one of us might make about our gender, age, size and weight, physical characteristics, sexual orientation. Not one meaningful statement emerges that is not reliant upon its 'not-self' counterparts. Any explicit statement about 'I', implicitly reveals 'not-I', just as, importantly, every explicit statement regarding 'not-I' (others) reveals implicit statements regarding 'I'.[5]

This interrelational grounding 'relocates' the self in the sense that our accessing of self does not emerge from looking 'within', but, rather, we can begin to discern that the self is revealed through, or between, the interrelationship of the being with the world. From this perspective, rather than being the originator or source of our experience of being, self emerges as a *product* or *outcome* of living as a human being. It comes forth, or stands out to our reflective awareness through particular acts of consciousness whose 'organizational meaning structure' is the self. Seen in this light, the self becomes the culmination of the attempt to shape or structure experience so that it is made meaningful from an object-based standpoint.[6]

Let me attempt to express this somewhat complex point in another way. Consider the following experiences: long-distance running, meditation, orgasm, being 'really caught up' in reading a book, listening to music, gardening, feeling tired to the point of exhaustion. One crucial feature shared by all of these diverse experiences is that while immersed in them, our consciousness of being is focused upon the activity or the event. In such instances, the self, as we usually understand, shape or define it, is attenuated, or stretched far beyond its usual boundaries, or may be experienced as having been temporarily lost or 'set aside'.

On further consideration, the self only 'reappears' (or, somewhat less radically, our self-focused reflections upon experience regain their meaningfulness and centrality) once the activity or event has come to an end and is now the object of reflection. That is to say, it is in that shift from doing (or 'being immersed in') the activity to that of considering what we are, or have been doing, that the self emerges. Indeed, we are likely to know the effects of this shift all too well in those instances when we become 'self-conscious' *while in the midst of such activities*, with the result that they are diminished or are prevented from continuing.[7] We also recognize that these very same activities which share this ability to diminish or supersede our sense of self are also the most likely to be identified by us as being or providing the most significant, memorable, meaningful, pleasurable or generally life-engaging experiences in our lives. A paradox emerges: we seem to be being most 'ourselves' when our 'self' is least apparent.

The phenomenological view of self as an interrelational outcome constituent of lived experience may hold merit not merely as an abstract possibility. More importantly, it 'captures', at least in part, our reflective experiences of being. Through this radical shift in our assumptions regarding self, we can no longer subscribe to a view that conceives of the self as being either intrapsychically located, or able to be defined in isolation (as something 'in and of itself') or that it is the impetus to consciousness.

This same shift in perspective leads us to question the notion of the fixedness and stability of the self. For, if self is an interrelational outcome, then any shift in, or with, that with which the self is in relation will, of necessity, alter the self as well. Thus, for instance, if, through psychotherapy, I alter my perspective on an event in my remembered past, this relational shift will reconstitute my sense of who I am now and, in turn, this 'new I' will experience a different meaning relationship to the remembered past event, not only in terms of what is remembered (and, more precisely, what is viewed as being important in what is remembered) but also how the event is remembered in terms of attitudes, emotions, evaluative judgements, beliefs and so on.

Finally, with the loss of its fixedness and stability, the very notion of a unitary self is also challenged. While it may be the case that at any point in time we experience the self as being singular, this should not lead us to suppose that it is always *the same*, singular self that is being experienced. Rather, the implications of a phenomenological argument suggest the contrary.

If the self is neither constant nor singular can we properly speak of a 'true' self that can be distinguished from a 'false' one? In the sense that we refer to 'true' (or 'real') as being fixed essence categories that are distinguishable from another set of essence categories labelled 'false' (or 'unreal'), we cannot. However, we might instead suggest that what we seek to express in terms of 'true' and 'false' relies upon a far more fluid interrelational sense of experience; namely that, reflectively speaking, we can to some degree distinguish our reflections on experience as being 'true' or 'real' to the experience insofar as these, at least in part, correspond to accurate expressions of that which is being reflectively experienced. Similarly, we might distinguish those reflections upon experience which deviate from, deny or seek to replace that which we are experiencing as examples of 'false' or 'unreal' reflections upon the self, but this has nothing to do with the truth or falseness of any given aspect or expression of self. Rather the focus is upon the being's willingness or unwillingness to reflect upon the self that is made present through the current act of self-reflection.

Again, a simple concrete example should clarify this last point. A particular event presents me with the reflective experience 'I am angry', but, instead of accepting this 'true' reflective experience, I transform it so that it becomes a 'false' reflective experience (such as 'I couldn't care less' or 'I am not the least bit angry'). In this sense, the 'real' angry reflective self is replaced or swamped by an 'unreal' disinterested or not angry reflective self.

Some existentially minded colleagues might present examples such as this as instances of self-deception.[8] I can see the appeal in such a conclusion, but personally I find this solution to be unsatisfactory. It does not seem to me to be so much an instance of self-deception as that of limited self-reflection. More accurately, we could state: 'I am angry but I cannot be, so I am telling myself that I couldn't care less and that I am not the least bit angry'. While this distinction might at first seem to be somewhat pedantic, I will seek to demonstrate below that this alternative provides us with significant clarifications regarding the self that would be more difficult to grasp if we retain the first option. Whatever the preference, however, it becomes apparent that a phenomenologically derived perspective challenges all seven of the dominant Western assumptions about the self that have been outlined above. None the less, it remains the case that such challenges have not yet been seriously considered by most psychotherapists.

Why are psychotherapists so resistant to these alternatives? While the reasons are likely to be many, I would suggest that one dominant reason is that if they were to accept them, many of the foundational assumptions that maintain their theoretical models would become untenable. I will return to this point in Chapter 4 (which deals with the pivotal foundational assumption concerning the unconscious), but, for now, I wish to focus the remainder of this chapter upon a psychotherapeutically relevant way of considering the issues of the self that tend to be brought by clients from a phenomenologically derived standpoint.

Let me begin by pointing out a recurring *language-based*

dilemma regarding all such enterprises. The very attempt to write about the self from an interactive interrelational standpoint accentuates the (probably) insuperable problems raised by the English language itself (and, perhaps to varying degrees, all languages). English, as a language, appears to be founded upon an attitude of 'having' or 'ownership' that, as a result, sometimes obviously, at times more subtly, forces upon us a world-view that is *essence-focused*. As such, no matter how forcefully we seek to convey the notion of 'self as interactive process', the word 'self' defies our very enterprise by asserting its 'it-ness' or 'thing-ness' which, in turn, creates confusing and apparently contradictory communications. One might seek to circumvent these difficulties by speaking of 'self-in-relation' or some other, somewhat unwieldy term, or, following the example of Martin Heidegger, by inventing new terms such as 'dasein'.[9] Unfortunately, in order to define what such novel terms might mean, the metaphors required bring us straight back to the very terms we seek to avoid. As such, I have suggested an alternative, if still inadequate, strategy that is somewhat less unwieldy and contains the added bonus of responding to a further, no less significant problem that will become more apparent in the discussion below. My position, in brief, is as follows.

As well as being conscious creatures, human beings display a particular focus of consciousness that can be labelled 'self-consciousness'. That is to say, not only are we gifted with the ability to exist in the world in a 'knowing' or 'meaning-construing manner', but also one specific if not dominant means available to us through which to know the world emerges from a self-reflective, or self-aware, standpoint. How consciousness or *self-consciousness* emerge, and what necessary conditions are required for their emergence, remains the topic of a great deal of speculation and controversy. Numerous theories put forward by philosophers, psychologists, cognitive scientists and spiritual leaders exist, but at present none is entirely satisfactory. The hypotheses and debates are fascinating and worth examining. However, they remain outside the boundaries of this chapter.[10] At present, therefore, just as we cannot fully understand, locate, describe or identify consciousness in general, so, too, is it the case for self-consciousness. It follows from this last point that the 'self-constituent' of self-consciousness is also, at present, largely a mystery.

And yet, while we are left largely with unproven speculations about the self, at the same time, from the standpoint of reflective experience, the self – our experience of each of us as a self – remains a relatively constant invariant of being human. As stated above, what we label as the 'self' is the means by which we give focus, shape and meaning to our reflections upon our experience of existing. However adequate these metaphors may appear to be, no metaphor can fully capture that which is being considered. As such, our statements about 'self' are, more properly, statements about how we have given metaphorical meaning and structure to our reflective experience of self (and self-consciousness).

While we cannot really study or capture self, we can make statements about what constitutes the *self-structure* each of us maintains in order to bring (self-consciously focused) meaning to our experience of living.

Why might speaking about a self-structure be less problematic than that of considering 'the self'? First, because it makes plain that what we refer to is a metaphorical construct intended to address, in part, a fluid, process-like experience of being human rather than leading us to suppose that this fluid process is some more static 'thing', or entity. Second, because it brings our focus back to a discourse that is concerned with our embodied experience of being self-aware. Third, it allows us to address a seeming contradiction arising from phenomenological analyses of the self: namely, that the 'self' which is postulated as being an interrelational fluid process is none the less experienced by us from an essence-based standpoint. That is to say, in my moment-to-moment reflective experience of 'being me', I do not experience my 'self' as an interrelational fluid process but, rather, as a relatively fixed essence: me. The term 'self-structure' serves to contain this (apparent) contradiction and, to some degree at least, permit further investigation from a standpoint that acknowledges this experiential variability rather than insisting upon the inadequate strategy of endorsing one standpoint and denying the experiential relevance of the other. Finally, while this term remains somewhat clumsy, it allows us to minimize our reliance upon terms such as 'self', 'myself', 'ourselves', and so on – all of which would suggest an inherently essentialist structure. Sadly, these attempts fail to free us completely from this tendency. Unavoidable terms like 'I' and 'me' continue to be required – at least until someone far more creative than 'me' comes up with suitable alternatives.

The self-structure contains and expresses a number of typically recurring, 'fixed structural patterns' or *sedimentations* in a person's way of engaging with the world from an object-focused standpoint. These sedimentations provide the self-structure with a sense of (relatively) fixed and permanent essence.

The problems that arise through sedimentations of the self-structure, insofar as they are of relevance to psychotherapy, can be summarized briefly: the self-reflective experiences arising from our interactions with others, or the world in general, may not 'fit' the recurring structural patterns of fixed values, attitudes, behavioural stances and beliefs which sediment the self-structure. Or, to put it another way, the sedimented self-structure is continually challenged as a result of its interrelational meetings with the world.

In these circumstances of dissonance or inadequacy of meaning, two principal options become available: either the self-structure is opened to these challenges so that some particular aspect of the self-structure is re-construed (or de-sedimented and re-sedimented anew as a different structure), or the existing self-structure is maintained via a particular strategy of *dissociation* of the challenging interrelational experience either in part or as a whole.

Each strategy has its experiential consequences. The recurring adoption of the first strategy provokes an increasing inability to sufficiently contain and define the self-structure. The more open the self-structure is to 'reflective experience as it is lived' the less sedimented it becomes and, as a consequence, the less definable or identifiable and provoking of uncertainty and unease. Taking up the second strategy in a rigid fashion designed to (over)protect the existing self-structure creates ever more inflexibility in the self-structure so that it requires a disidentification with or dissociation from all lived experiences that destabilize it. This, in turn, is likely to be experienced as restrictions in thought, affect or behaviour that are expressed in phrases like 'I feel so empty or dead inside' or 'I feel like a robot that is just going through the motions'.

That our more typical chosen stance relies upon the second option is made more explicable when we realize that *the opening of any aspect or element of the self-structure to challenge alters the whole of the self-structure.* A telling example provided by Emmy van Deurzen serves to clarify this point (though it must be stated that this should in no way lead anyone to suppose that she is in agreement with the hypotheses being put forward).

In a paper dealing with the self,[11] van Deurzen focuses upon the experience of her client, Rosa. In brief, Rosa's struggle *'with a strong infatuation which had taken over every aspect of her life'*[12] challenged her self-structure with regard to its sedimented values and beliefs concerning 'being an independent woman', 'maintaining a reserve towards emotional relations with men', and so on, all of which significantly challenged the totality of meaning that maintained this self-structure. With the assistance of her therapist, Rosa's self-structure became sufficiently less rigid ('de-sedimented') such that she became more open to her experience of challenges rather than continuing to close off to them via dissociative explanations that would allow maintenance of the previously existing self-structure. In other words, the therapeutic interaction permitted Rosa to question sedimented aspects of the self-structure under challenge and to re-create a more adequate self-structure.

Consider van Deurzen-Smith's statement with regard to what has just been suggested:

> It was Rosa's act of redefining this experience as one of getting to know herself as a new person that allowed her to stop suffering. In essence, Rosa reinterpreted her experience of selfhood as encompassing all the extremes of ups and downs, all the oscillations between aloneness and fusion with another. She had to resituate herself as a person capable of such breadth and flexibility and find peace in inhabiting a new universe, which was sometimes filled with glorious togetherness and at other times restricted to the narrow confines of her sorrow. When she learnt to accommodate the enormity of such experience, accepting it all as part of her, it stopped being torture to gain and lose her lover all the time, for in losing him she no longer lost herself. In practising the art of extending herself in this way Rosa discovered that she had broadened her basis of existence and that she had managed to achieve a better balance in every other aspect of her life through it. Her previously rather more narrowly defined sense of self was abandoned. Rosa spoke of having risen like a phoenix from her own ashes. She felt that she had survived the death of her former self.[13]

Now, it seems to me that there is nothing contained in this statement that would be lost to us if it were re-phrased from the standpoint of the self-structure. What would be gained, on the other hand, would be our ability to let go of terms such as 'getting to know herself', 'losing herself', 'extending herself', 'the death of a former self', and so forth – all of which impose upon us a viewpoint which stands contrary to the interrelational conclusions regarding 'self' espoused by existential psychotherapy.

Let me now turn my attention towards the notion of *dissociation* within the context of the self-structure. Dissociation, as I employ the term, does *not* refer to the avowed 'division' or 'splitness' of 'self', 'personality' or 'intrapsychic entities', nor is it meant to suggest notions of 'subpersonalities' – be they multiple, semi-autonomous, or concurrently existing. Rather, my focus upon dissociation seeks to clarify that 'splitness in reflective being' that arises when the self-structure's response to the challenges of meeting the world is that of denying or 'disowning' those challenges in order that the current sedimentations which define it can be maintained. In this way, such challenging interrelational experiences are 'blocked' or remain unassimilated as new aspects or expressions of the self-structure. Nevertheless, they must be 'explained'. Typical explanations assume the existence of alien agencies, be they natural or supernatural, internal or external, that temporarily overwhelm or possess the self-structure and replace it with an alien construct. R. D. Laing's notions of *engulfment, implosion and petrification* encapsulate these explanations in typically vivid fashion.[14] In short, experiential dissociation expresses a fundamental unwillingness to carry through with the challenges of meeting the world in order to safeguard the stability of the sedimented self-structure.

Once again, a brief example from my own psychotherapeutic practice should make clear what is being suggested. Louise, a supermarket cashier, believes that she is – and must be – always honest and truthful, but, at the same time, Louise confesses to me that she steals money from her till on a regular basis so that she and her boyfriend, Adam, can go out clubbing on weekends. In order that Louise's sedimented self-structure ('I must be honest and truthful') can continue to be maintained, it is required, in turn, to deny or disown those challenging experiences that contradict or challenge it (stealing money). As such, Louise 'explains' these occurrences in terms of 'I'm being made to by Adam and he has a powerful hold on me'. Via this explanation, Louise can continue to preserve her existing self-structure – but at a price. Certain interrelational experiences have been, and must continue to be, dissociated such that she does not experience herself to be in control of various aspects of her thoughts, affects and behaviours identified with the dissociated experiences.

As such, while this view of dissociation focuses upon those same phenomena that are more commonly understood in terms of the hypotheses of polypsychism, Dissociative Identity Disorders (DID) or Multiple Personality Disorders (MPD), it avoids their increasingly problematic assumption that requires the existence of multiple entities or 'essences' (or, indeed, a singular essence). Instead, self-structure dissociations expose split stances between one's reflective experiences and one's judgemental beliefs about these experiences, and therefore remain within the boundaries of a common human interrelational process.

Some further relevant clarifications now become necessary. There is every reason to suppose that the self-structure can 'hold' or 'incorporate' complementary, co-existing, even contradictory values and beliefs. What remains crucial is that whether or not certain values and beliefs are held, all are owned or identified with that self-structure. Van Deurzen's study of her client, Rosa, serves as a good example of this in that, via her therapy, Rosa found the ability to acknowledge and respect complex, even contradictory, ways of being and to hold them within her re-created self-structure. Such a circumstance strikes me as being not at all unusual even if, of necessity, it opens or de-sediments the self-structure such that it becomes increasingly difficult to define its content, beliefs and values in a simplistic fashion. Indeed, this very incapacity to define the constituents of the self-structure in any final or fixed sense seems to me to be the crux of any movement towards what may be labelled authenticity.

The issue is not that the self-structure need be coherent or predictable, but rather, whether the self-structure is able to remain open to the challenges of interrelational existence. If the self-structure encounters experiential challenges that will not allow it to maintain certain fixed or sedimented stances, it has two options: the re-creation of the self-structure or dissociation.

An example provide by Mick Cooper serves to clarify this point.[15] 'Dr Jekyll' maintains a self-structure whose sedimented beliefs and values cannot own certain ways of being. These are dissociated and become characteristic features of an alien construct, (i.e. 'Mr Hyde'). In the same fashion, 'Mr Hyde' also maintains a self-structure whose sedimented beliefs and values cannot 'own' certain ways of being. These, too, are dissociated and become characteristic features of an 'alien construct' (i.e. 'Dr Jekyll'). Both constructs co-exist at the level of immediate experience but remain experientially dissociated at the level of reflection. We cannot assert that 'Dr Jekyll' is the 'real' being, just as we cannot assert that 'Mr Hyde' is. Both of them are 'real' in that they are part of the being's interrelational experience. As such, it is not the interrelational experience that is divided, but rather, it is the case that the being's reflections upon interrelational experience impose the belief of 'splitness' so that the sedimented 'Dr Jekyll' self-structure dissociates the sedimented, and 'alien', 'Mr Hyde' construct, and vice versa.

At each moment of dissociated experience, however, the belief will be held that one sedimented construct is the self-structure while the other is the alien construct. Should the two constructs co-exist simultaneously as 'owned' aspects of either 'Dr Jekyll's' or 'Mr Hyde's' self-structure, then a novel self-structure (incorporating both) will have emerged. Is this not what those who believe in multiple personalities seek to suggest when they speak of 'integrating the multiple selves'?

Once again, this phenomenologically derived hypothesis of the self-construct asserts that any given self-structure is a reflective product of, and not the source-point to, experience. In other words, the self-structure emerges through reflection rather than being the directive agent of reflection. As such, at each moment of reflection a self-structure emerges which may be simple or complex, coherent or contradictory. But that which the self-structure expresses is a reflectively derived, possibly deeply held, set of beliefs and values regarding inter-relational experience – *not* experience itself. In all cases, what I would consider to be of import is whether the self-structure which emerges within that reflective moment remains open to its experience of the various interrelational focus modalities as were discussed in Chapter 2.

As a final point, let me inject a note a caution. From a psychotherapeutic perspective, it must be stressed that it is essential to begin any exploration and challenge of the client's existing self-structure by acknowledging and respecting the possibility that, however limiting to the client's experience of living the dissociative dictates that maintain the construct may be, these may still express the only strategy currently available to the client in order that some sense of life stability and meaning – no matter how tenuous – is permitted. In such circumstances, the psychotherapist's insistence upon manipu-lating the self-structure (no matter how well intentioned and ameliorative this may appear to be) might well succeed in provoking far greater psychic damage. The awareness of this possibility is particularly apparent in working with those cli-ents who have been diagnosed as exhibiting extreme mental disorders.

I will extend my discussion on the self-structure and the co-existent modalities of sedimentation and dissociation in

Chapter 4. For now, if my overall argument can be expressed in its most direct form, I believe that this can be summarized in the underlying 'moral' so beautifully conveyed in Kurt Vonnegut's novel *Mother Night*: '*Be careful who you pretend to be. For who you pretend to be is who you are.*'[16]

4 Do we really need the unconscious?

Nearly a decade ago now, I wrote a paper entitled 'The unconscious: an idea whose time has gone?' which was subsequently published in the *Journal of the Society for Existential Analysis* and, later, in the Society's first collection of outstanding papers.[1] As its title suggests, my thesis sought to reconsider psychotherapy's overwhelming acceptance of, and reliance upon, the psychoanalytically derived hypothesis of a particular and distinct mental system – the unconscious – whose active influence upon our lives (as we enact and consciously reflect upon them) was both substantial and requiring of primary attention by psychoanalysts and psychotherapists. In addition, my paper attempted to provide an alternative means to understand, and work with psychotherapeutically, all the experiential phenomena upon which the hypothesis of the unconscious rests, and that have been felt, observed and discussed by psychotherapists and their clients. This alternative means relies upon the interrelated notions of *sedimentation* and *dissociation* that were discussed in Chapter 3.

I had no idea, at the time of writing, of the degree to which this paper would provoke strong emotional responses, ranging from uninhibited joy to near-violent rage. I have had the experience of weeping psychoanalysts 'confessing' to me (always privately, of course) of the 'loss of faith' which they had suffered in silence for years and, equally, I have been publicly condemned by colleagues for having provided a further coffinnail to the ever-lengthening line of critics and detractors of psychotherapy by calling into question one of the primary and unquestionable principles of our profession.

Of the first reaction I can say very little; of the latter, however, it remains important to me to state the following: Freud remains in my heart as my mentor, hero, and intellectual father-figure. I count myself as one of his many heirs who, however rebellious, retains the deepest respect and gratitude for the many and profound contributions he has made and which continue to enrich and challenge our lives. It is, I believe, in the spirit of enquiry that exemplifies much of Freud's work that I have presented my thesis. As to the extreme reactions mentioned above, I continue to shake my head in wonder and dismay; what an odd line of work I find myself in.

None the less, over the years, as well, it has become apparent to me that some of the points argued in my paper have been misunderstood, or not sufficiently understood with regard to their implications, and, more commonly, that my attempts to present a case against the unconscious did not discuss some further concerns that have, for me, become more pressing. Thus, while the essential argument has not been substantially altered, my intent in this chapter is to present a clearer, more adequate and succinct discussion on a topic that, if anything, thanks to the continuing 'Freud Wars' with which psychotherapy has been encumbered in recent years, has become more pertinent to the development of theory and to considerations of practice.

In his brilliant *Introductory Lectures On Psycho-analysis*, Sigmund Freud presented his now famous challenge to psychology with regard to the reality of the unconscious:

> **We challenge anyone in the world to give a more correct scientific account of this state of affairs, and if he does we will gladly renounce our hypothesis of unconscious mental processes. Until that happens, however, we will hold fast to the hypothesis;**

> **and if someone objects that here the unconscious is nothing real**
> **in a scientific sense, is a makeshift, *une façon de parler*, we can**
> **only shrug our shoulders resignedly and dismiss what he says as**
> **unintelligible.**[2]

This was quite a claim for even a self-confessed 'conquistador' of science to make, but, what did he actually mean? What was this 'hypothesis of unconscious mental processes' to which he referred? What were its underlying assumptions and implications? What did Freud mean by 'unconscious'? Let me attempt a brief summary.

There continues to exist a fair degree of confusion as to Freud's meaning and use of the term 'the unconscious' since he significantly revised his ideas no less than three times and formally presented the unconscious in 'at least three formally acknowledged senses – the "descriptive", "dynamic" and "systemic"'.[3]

In its descriptive sense, Freud's unconscious is any mental system that exists outside of our consciousness. It might include the wide gamut of repressed material stressed by psychoanalysis, but extends beyond this set of conditions to cover all non-conscious mental activity. In its dynamic sense, the Freudian unconscious refers to a further distinction made by Freud in which he hypothesizes two types of unconscious: the preconscious and the unconscious proper. The preconscious is distinguished by the ease with which its material may be made conscious. If, for instance, in the course of a discussion about a television programme we have both watched I unexpectedly ask you to tell me your mother's maiden name and you are able to do so, that 'material' can be said to have existed in the preconscious and was 'brought to consciousness' with little difficulty. The unconscious proper, however, is characterized by the difficulty (if not impossibility) of its material being brought to consciousness, other than via disguised or symbolic means or, as it is argued, via the impact of psychoanalytic interventions.

The systemic unconscious is perhaps best explained in the following passage by David Livingstone Smith whose expository eloquence on all matters relating to Freudian theory is a refreshing alternative to the more usual obscurantist ramblings of the great majority of his psychoanalytic colleagues. Smith writes that via

> The *System Ucs* . . . Freud attempted to set out the relationship between such mental processes as memory, perception and consciousness; account for dreams parapraxes and psychoneurotic symptoms; and through which he attempted to discern the main functional units of the mind . . .
>
> The mind is composed of three systems. The unconscious system thinks, in a way, but is unable to link up its thoughts with language. It can represent things concretely, but cannot represent relationships between things or abstract properties from objects (it cannot represent 'universals') – both of which require some form of language. In the *System Ucs* ideas are linked associatively rather than logically. They evoke rather than entail one another.
>
> In order to become conscious, an unconscious idea must first become linked with language. The part of the mind where language is kept is called the preconscious system. Once unconscious items get linked up with the appropriate sentences they become preconscious, and this is a necessary but not a sufficient condition for their becoming conscious. . .
>
> An idea becomes conscious by impacting on a third system, the conscious system. . .
>
> According to Freud, repression occurs at the node between the unconscious and preconscious systems. As a nonlogical system, the unconscious part of the mind cannot experience conflict. However, when unconscious items enter the

> preconscious system – with its logico-linguistic structure – they can give rise to conflict and therefore distress. Repression is said to occur when an unconscious item is denied access to language – is literally not given a voice – because of the conflicts which would arise if it were to find preconscious representation. So repression does not create the unconscious. It just prevents an unconscious item from becoming anything more than unconscious.[4]

Unfortunately, these various and at times complex distinctions regarding the psychoanalytic unconscious are not always so clearly delineated (and, I suggest, understood) by those psychotherapists who both utilize and rely upon the term. To be fair, Freud himself confounds matters throughout his writings. For example, he tells us that *'Psychoanalysis was forced, through the study of pathological repression, to take the concept of the "unconscious" seriously.'*[5] This would appear to suggest that the primary issue for Freud is the notion of repression and that it is repression, more than anything else, that makes the debates surrounding an unconscious system of any importance to psychotherapists.

With regard to repression, Peter Gay, a recent major biographer sympathetic to Freud's theory, states: *'Most of the unconscious consists of repressed materials ... the unconscious proper resembles a maximum-security prisoner holding antisocial inmates languishing for years or recently arrived, inmates harshly treated and heavily guarded, but barely kept under control and forever attempting to escape.'*[6]

This idea that we all maintain in our minds unconscious memories, images, desires and wishes that are denied direct, undisguised access to our conscious thoughts (or, as Smith puts it, are denied access to language) holds tremendous fascination for many – not least those of us who, as psychotherapists or clients, engage in psychotherapeutic discourse. A major part of that fascination, of course, lies in the connected idea that, were we to bring to consciousness at least some of this repressed material, a great many of the mysteries, conflicts and oddities that we encounter in our daily thoughts and actions, oddities which taunt and mystify and disempower us, would be explained, and, through explanation, diminish or disappear altogether. It is all too easy – and tempting – to experience the power of this idea and to lend it credence. None the less, if, as so many psychotherapists claim, 'we are seekers of truth', we cannot afford to be beguiled by attractive but problematic 'belief systems'. It is now right and proper that I should attempt to express my concerns and critiques of the principal ideas summarized thus far. I will follow this with an outline of an alternative perspective.

The great majority of psychoanalysts, and psychotherapists in general, argue that the most significant evidence for their theories and hypotheses is that which emerges from their psychotherapeutic work with clients. While being a troublesome notion of 'evidence', I am in general agreement with them. My own view is that the knowledge-base of contemporary psychotherapy is at a prescientific level and, as such, all data gathered from the enterprise itself is invaluable. In this spirit then, I begin my critique by recounting once again my 'ur-tale' of how I, a true believer in the psychoanalytic unconscious, came to lose my 'faith'.

My client, June, had come to me desperate to rid herself of nightly disturbances which prevented her from maintaining undisturbed sleep lasting anything more than about an hour. June's inability to sleep for prolonged periods of time had begun not long after the age of 13 (she was 22 years old when she began therapy with me). June believed that the problem had to do with the fact that she could not dream.

June explained that each time she began to dream (or, more correctly, each time she remembered *beginning* to dream) she would 'see' the same startling image that would immediately bring her to wakefulness. This image was that of a chessboard, or so it seemed to June, since it consisted of a pattern of dark- and light-coloured squares symmetrically laid out so that they followed one another. Even just talking about this image induced for June feelings of anxiety, fear, dizziness and nausea.

Eventually, following an analytically attuned series of sessions, June realized that the disturbing image was not that of a chessboard at all, but rather was her family's linoleum-tiled basement floor that had been patterned with red and white squares. With this realization, she was able to remember that during her thirteenth year, when she had been in the room one afternoon, a male friend of her older brother had forced her to fellate him. She had never told anyone of the event and, indeed, had 'forgotten' it until now.

The next time I saw her, June informed me that she had had her first undisturbed sleep in years and had actually managed to dream a proper dream. Soon after, our sessions together ended. As far as I was concerned, the most adequate means with which to understand June's problems was to conclude that she had *repressed* the event by allowing it to express itself only in consciousness in the disguised and innocuous image of a chessboard which, nevertheless, provoked strong emotional and physical – if seemingly inexplicable – reactions.

However, some weeks later, June asked to see me again. No, her disturbances had not begun again; in fact, she was sleeping well and had come to terms with the assault. But there was something she needed to confess. She had not *truly* repressed the event. Instead, she had been aware of it, but in a detached and disconnected fashion, as if it both was and was not in her thoughts. Or, to put it another way, it was like a thought that did not belong to her. June's words contained a disturbing idea for me that I could not dismiss, not least because it captured much of my own experiences of 'making the unconscious conscious'. The revelatory material had not actually been hidden or repressed; rather, somehow, it had become *disowned* such that in some way the 'I' who knew the material and the 'I' to whom the material belonged were somehow separate, seemingly dissociated.

It was this shift in perspective, from that relying upon a psychoanalytic assumption regarding separate and distinct mental systems to that of a self-structure-imposed dividedness in one's conscious experience that provided the key to reformulating the unconscious. None the less, it is essential to stress from the outset that this critique of the psychoanalytic unconscious does not call into question, nor attempt to deny, the lived experience of insight or 'connection' that is usually explained as 'the unconscious made conscious'. What is of concern here is the adequacy of this explanation. Is this really the most satisfactory answer that psychotherapists can offer? I do not think so, for all manner of reasons.

First, an Occam's razor reason. The pivotal point upon which the hypothesis of the unconscious rests is that it must be seen as a separate and distinct system to that of consciousness. However, at this moment in time what we know of, or can state with any certainty, about consciousness is extremely limited. It is, for now, largely a mystery with regard to its definition, its 'location', its relationship to the brain, its extensions into our cognitive and behavioural processes.[7] The unconscious, too, assuming it exists, is also as intractable a mystery as consciousness. Confronted with such, does it make parsimonious sense to insist upon two distinct and separate systems when we can state next to nothing about either? It may well be that, some time in the future, sufficient data will emerge to allow us this distinction, or, alternatively, we may fail to discern any significant distinction. But, until then, would it not be wiser to consider the various phenomena gleaned from what we have assumed to be two separate systems as, possibly, expressions of a single, if still highly mysterious, system?

Second, I have no difficulty with the idea that at any point in time there exist mental activities of which a subject is not currently aware. Indeed, I think that it would be absurd for anyone to deny such an argument as there exists plentiful research evidence in favour of this view.[8] If this were all that the term 'unconscious' was meant to highlight, there would be nothing for me to dispute. Indeed, it was a view advocated long before Freud.

As L. L. Whyte reminds us, '*the idea of unconscious mental processes was, in many of its aspects, conceivable around 1700, topical around 1800, and became effective around 1900.*'[9] But how was this pre-Freudian version of the unconscious defined? Certainly, each of the many and varied philosophers, poets, scientists and medical doctors who employed the term did so within their unique and specific set of perspectives and aims, but broadly, all rested their claims upon the experiential assumption of mental processes that lay beyond (or beneath, or behind) those that make up our immediate, or current, awareness. As such, broadly speaking, the unconscious was a term employed to represent all mental activity other than '*those discrete aspects or brief phases which enter awareness as they occur.*'[10]

However, to accept this in no way forces us to conclude the existence of a separate intrinsic 'system unconscious'. Instead, it is generally accepted that those phenomena typically associated with such experiences form part of a single process system – consciousness – of which conscious awareness or attention forms a subset.[11]

Third, a somewhat obvious, but significant, logical problem: If we follow the arguments made by psychoanalysis regarding 'the unconscious proper', it becomes evident that we can never be certain that what we conclude to be 'the unconscious made conscious' actually *is* (or was ever) truly the unconscious. We cannot know in a conscious manner the unconscious content itself, since, to know it consciously makes it no longer unconscious. If so, how can we be certain that what we have declared to be previously unconscious material is not just another disguise designed to protect us from that which is truly unconscious material? The closed circularity of the psychoanalytic argument has no way of being broken; as such, its explanatory value is severely restricted.

Fourth, I point readers to Jean-Paul Sartre's critique of the unconscious[12] and, in particular, refer those interested to Betty Cannon's excellent review of this argument.[13] While Sartre's critique is many-layered and focused upon numerous related issues (and, to be fair, has problems of its own),[14] I want to focus upon a very brief summary of what may well be his most important criticism. Recall that Smith tells us that repression occurs at the interface between the preconscious and unconscious systems and that it is at this interface that the 'language' available to the preconscious system that could permit the unconscious 'a voice' is denied (that is to say, repressed). But, Sartre argues, in order for this mechanism of repression to be allowed to occur, there must already exist some prior preconscious awareness of the dangerous or unsuitable 'voice' such that the repressive 'censor' located at the node between the preconscious and the unconscious systems must already know (have the language) for the seemingly unknown (pre-language) unconscious system. As such, it is not that the material is unknown (i.e. unconscious) but, rather, that there exists a *pretence* of not-knowing (what Sartre terms 'bad faith') at a conscious, if unattended (or, as Sartre prefers to label it, *unreflected*) level. Hence, there exists no need for a repression mechanism or, for that matter, for the unconscious.

All right, the reader might respond, but this still does not address the odd phenomena reported by numerous psychotherapists – the illogical associations, the sudden connections in meaning and affect, the remembering of seemingly lost material – of their clients' experiences. Are these and other related phenomena not predicted elements of the unconscious? Are they not critical factors in favour of its definition? While I must leave some of my answer until later, my fifth argument seeks to address these concerns. Again, it warns us that the hypothesis of the unconscious did not predict these phenomena, rather it sought to explain them. In similar fashion, the defining properties of the unconscious were not hypothesized prior to any observation; they arose as attempts to make sense of what was being observed and described. As to the associative phenomena specifically mentioned, might they not be as likely to present themselves as manifestations of a diffused, yet highly alert and observant conscious process brought about through the psychotherapeutic enterprise itself? How often does any one of us spend an hour of uninterrupted attention to our conscious thought processes? Is not such an exercise likely to provoke unusual associations, sudden connections in meaning and affect, a more vivid and accurate remembering of significant material from various points in our life experience? If so, who can state with certainty that the emergent phenomena *must* have arisen from a separate mental system?

Sixth, besides the data gathered from clinical material, what research evidence exists that might indicate the existence of a psychoanalytic unconscious? Here, those in favour of the unconscious hypothesis begin to wave their arms excitedly and direct us towards what might be seen initially at least to be strong suggestive evidence derived from experimental studies on subliminal perception, or preconscious processing, as made famous by Norman Dixon[15] and, as well, the startling data obtained from commissurotomy ('split-brain') studies[16] and other neuropsychological research studies. Those who are more up to date with regard to cognitive science research might also remind us that quite a few contemporary cognitive scientists conceptualize some workings of the mind in terms of unconscious processes.[17] Surely, there is no dispute here?

Well. . . Actually what is revealed here is an intellectual 'sleight of hand' being played out. All the above studies and assertions might well be seen to point to some sort of unconscious system, but what sort exactly? Recall that in its dynamic expression, Freud spoke of a distinction between material which is difficult to access but not repressed (the 'preconscious') and material which is both difficult to access and repressed (the 'unconscious proper'). In spite of what many psychoanalysts assert, all the above studies pointed to as evidence for the unconscious proper actually provide evidence for something akin to the preconscious which, I remind readers, most clearly mirrors previous pre-Freudian formulations of an unconscious that easily lend themselves to being analysed, today, as manifestations of consciousness. As such, while, at best, this research might be said to provide at least some suggestive evidence for unconscious processing, this unconscious processing bears little resemblance to the kind that is so pivotal to psychoanalytic theory.

Further, cognitive scientists' use of the term 'unconscious' often reveals a lack of clarity, or 'conceptual looseness' as to the meaning they give to this term such that it might be being employed in order to refer to a separate system or, alternatively, may be a 'shorthand' way for them to address issues concerning attention and awareness. For, just as attention studies, for instance, demonstrate that whatever stimuli we are aware of, or are mentally attuned to, at any moment in time are but a minute amount of all the stimuli being perceptually processed by our brain, we can make a distinction between those stimuli of which we are currently conscious (to which we attend) and those that are perceived in an unaware – or unconscious – fashion.[18]

However, this use of the terms 'conscious' and 'unconscious' bears only the vaguest similarity to the meanings that psychoanalysts place upon them. Nevertheless, in the great majority of cases, it is the non-psychoanalytic meaning of the terms upon which cognitive scientists focus their research. In this way, it is arguable that their studies are concerned more with differing or 'divided' functions attributable to a single mental system rather than being allied to psychoanalytic hypotheses of a distinct and separate system.

Part of the problem, of course, lies with the term 'unconscious' itself in that its plasticity of meaning permits it to express a wide range of possible definitions ranging from 'non-consciousness' (as in 'I was knocked unconscious') to that of one or more discrete mental processes other than conscious processing. The problem is further exacerbated by the employment of alternate terms such as 'subconscious', 'preconscious' (in the Dixonian sense) and so forth which, while originally coined in order to impose a formal distinction from that of the psychoanalytic unconscious, now appear to be employed either as synonyms for, or watered-down versions of, the psychoanalytic unconscious.

Seventh: What about the evidence in favour of repression? Surely, this hypothetical construct, so closely linked to the broader concept of the unconscious, might well settle the matter.

As well as many adherents, the concept of repression has had numerous critics. Early behaviourists merely expunged it from their vocabulary, while logical-positivist philosophers such as Wittgenstein[19] attacked its logical inconsistencies. Freud himself constantly revised and updated his definition in order to emphasize his broader concept of defence mechanisms, which subsumes the notion of repression.[20] Nevertheless, the principal gist of the notion remained much the same and continues to be employed (if for often competing and contradictory reasons) by all manner of advocates of the hypothesis. Problematically, however, in spite of all the attention and scrutiny it has been given, empirical evidence for repression remains highly inconclusive, and more straightforward alternative explanations for the phenomena that serve to define it continue to be put forward by researchers and practitioners alike.[21]

It is, principally, on the basis of these seven arguments that I have come to reject the notion of the unconscious as utilized by psychoanalysts and the great majority of psychotherapists. In contrast to their views, I will now put forward an alternative derived from what I earlier referred to as my 'ur-story'.

In Chapter 3 I proposed the idea of *the self-structure* and the interrelated notions of *sedimentation* and *dissociation*. I would now like to consider this hypothesis as an alternative way of making sense of those phenomena which have been utilized as providing the basis to the psychoanalytic unconscious.

Freud's initial attempts to make sense of those patients who *seemed* to have no access to parts of their mental life led him to propose the existence of an unconscious and that, in spite of the many revisions and clarifications he would continue to make with regard to this theory, it was this very 'splitness' or dissociation within the human psyche that remained as the fundamental rationale for his concept. I believe that Freud was profoundly correct not only in pursuing this question but also in retaining the centrality of this idea throughout the many reworkings of his theory. However, as James S. Grotstein has recently remarked, Freud's error was that he took the horizontal splits of the hysterics' double consciousness and, in effect, rotated them to the vertical plane, thereby superimposing the system consciousness atop the System Unconsciousness.[22]

Approaching this same issue from an alternative perspective, I would suggest that the 'splitness' under consideration expresses the dissonance between one's sedimentations regarding the self-structure – namely, who I insist I am, (and am not), who I can (and cannot) be, who I must (and must not) be – and the resulting dissociations from one's actual experience of being that will inevitably arise when one's experience of being fails to 'fit' these sedimentations. In brief, the dilemma arises when there is a conflict between, broadly speaking, one's beliefs about who one is (one's epistemological stance) and one's experience of being (one's phenomenological experience).

In such circumstances, two main options designed to resolve the conflict become available: alter the epistemological stance (that is to say, de-sediment that part of the self-structure that does not 'fit' one's lived experience of being and re-sediment a more adequate epistemological stance, *or* maintain the existing sedimented self-structure and reject, *or* 'disown' the conflicting experience. Each option has its problematic consequences. To adopt the former will threaten the whole of the existing sedimented self-structure since to modify any part of the sedimented self-structure is to alter the whole of it. Such a strategy will be experienced as being unsettling, anxiety-provoking, a movement towards increased existential uncertainty and insecurity regarding one's sense of identity. The alternative solution may well allay all these insecurities, but its price will be that one will now be doomed to experience at least part of one's life 'as if it were not mine'; that, in short, I will sometimes experience life from the standpoint of a being who has been 'possessed' by an alien agency that acts under its own impetus and demands and over which I have little, if any, control. This sense of an invasive alien 'otherness' can be viewed as having a natural or supernatural genesis or as being a product of a 'disease or sickness' within the individual or more properly belonging to society as a whole. Whatever the case, the issue is not that the disturbing and alienating material remains unremembered, but, rather, that it is disowned from the self-structure.

It is this second, more common, option that can be seen to 'thrive upon' and express those phenomena that have been the basis for the hypothesis of the psychoanalytic unconscious. By implication, we can begin to understand that the client's often courageous struggles in psychotherapy need not be seen as resistances to the possibility of 'the unconscious being made conscious' but might be more adequately seen as attempts to face not only the challenges of confronting the dissonance between the 'I' that I *say* is me and the 'I' who structures my experience, but, also of confronting the experience of increasing existential unease and insecurity being provoked by the de-sedimenting of the self-structure via the challenges of psychotherapeutic enquiry.

Importantly, however, this alternative hypothesis does not require the additional conjecture of an intrinsically different and separate mental system, since what dissonances and divisions might be said to exist are not in themselves divisions in consciousness itself, but rather are subjectively interpreted divisions designed to maintain an inadequately constructed self-structure. The divisions in (self-) consciousness are apparent, but not actual. Second, this alternative argument does not require the added conjecture of repression-based inaccessibility. Rather, one's experience is that one can 'know' or be aware of 'being a being who I claim I am not' (or maintaining desires, wishes, memories, etc. which I claim I do not maintain) with the proviso that this being, or those desires, wishes, memories, etc. belong to an alien other who is not who one claims to be, but who none the less 'takes over my being' and whose power and ability to enact that take-over is beyond 'my' control.

Does this hypothesis not fit far more adequately the lived experience of hypothesized 'unconscious mechanisms' and of 'making the unconscious conscious'? I would argue that it does, and that its greater adequacy rests, in part, upon its ability to respond to the seven objections to the hypothesis of the unconscious which were summarized above without rejecting or transforming their experiential basis.

Further, unlike the problem of evidence faced by advocates of the psychoanalytic unconscious, this alternative hypothesis can provide – admittedly indirect – collaborative research evidence. For the sake of brevity, I will outline a few of the more obvious examples.

Selective attention studies from experimental psychology have demonstrated that the principal factors which determine whether we will attend to certain sensory stimuli as opposed to myriad competing stimuli include both the physical characteristics of a stimulus (i.e. its size, movement, contrast and intensity) and a wide number of psychological factors such as our motives and expectations, our current mood and our past experiences.[23] Such studies demonstrate a fundamental, indeed cognitively necessary, mechanism of dissociation whereby the vast majority of sensory stimuli that, while open to conscious awareness, remain on its periphery in order to permit a minute minority of stimuli to form the focus of our attention. Everyday experience demonstrates to us not only that we select experiential material for the purposes of reflection, but also that, in many circumstances, novel instances of awareness or insight occur when we reflect upon material that was previously on the periphery of our awareness. Much of the pleasure derived from crime and mystery novels, for example, rests precisely upon the detective's ability to suddenly 'see' what had always been there but which had previously escaped his or her (and everyone else's) attention.

In a similar way, the large number of replicated experiments on *subliminal perception* (or, to employ Norman Dixon's more recent terminology, *preconscious processing*,[24]) attest to the fact that a great deal of information available to us remains at an *unattended* level. In summarizing various experiments on the recoverability of subliminal stimuli into attended consciousness carried out with several colleagues, Matthew Erdelyi concludes that the evidence obtained does reveal the subject's '*willingness to report uncertain recollections*'.[25] Such studies suggest that material initially unattended to, and thus seemingly unavailable to conscious recall, can, via focused attention (thought), become reflectively conscious.

Proprioceptive dysfunctions (i.e. disorders) in the recognition of one's body definitions and boundaries, can also be seen to provide fascinatingly collaborative evidence. Both Jonathan Miller[26] and Oliver Sacks[27] supply telling examples of variations in proprioception in a number of stroke victims who *disown* parts of their bodies (usually their limbs) and will produce the most outlandish explanations to account for the 'alien' limbs that have seemingly become attached to them. These cases can, I think, be best understood in the light of a point made earlier in this chapter; namely, that such dysfunctions reveal a conflict between epistemological beliefs and phenomenological experience. That is, that while the patient might eventually be convinced to accept or believe the evidence that the limbs are his or her own, his or her experience of ownership nevertheless remains dissociated. Opposite circumstances, such as the phenomenon of *the phantom limb*, can be understood in the same way. Once again, these examples of psychophysical dissociation are paralleled in the more clearly psychological dissociations implicit (or explicit) in the statements of clients who might, for example, believe that the sexual abuse of children is wrong and unacceptable but who experience themselves as being 'seduced' by their victims.

Finally, studies of psychologically based dissociative phenomena such as *dissociated identity disorders* (or what was once termed *multiple personality disorders*) provide obvious parallells to the sedimented/dissociated self-structure discussed above. Stephen Braude's *First Person Plural: Multiple Personality and the Philosophy of Mind*[28] and Ian Hacking's *Rewriting the Soul: Multiple Personality and the Sciences of Memory*[29] both provide substantive aetiologies of the development of these disorders and present the case both for and against their acceptance in a fair-minded fashion.

As was argued in Chapter 3, phenomenologically derived analyses place the focus of dissociation upon the self-structure's 'ownership' or 'disownership' of reflective experience rather than considering the issue from the standpoint of polypsychism or multiple personalities. This realignment of focus removes the most significant problems and contradictions associated with these disorders.

The perspective of 'divided consciousness' that has been put forward as an alternative to that of a psychoanalytic unconscious also provides the psychotherapist with a significantly different attitudinal and methodological approach to his or her encounter with clients. First, it places the focus of psychotherapy upon the descriptive clarification of the client's current way of being so that the self-structure through which that being stance is expressed and maintained can be more adequately disclosed. Second, through this disclosure the therapist and client alike can begin to discern those qualitatively lived aspects of the self-structure that are most deeply sedimented, or fixed in such a fashion that they remain resistant to challenge and reconsideration by the client regardless of the restrictions upon the client's interrelational experience of being that their adoption imposes. Third, via the clarification of the client's sedimentations, various emergent distorted and disowned aspects can begin to be identified as experiential elements of the dissociated structure through which the client's self-structure is protected and maintained. Fourth, the examination of the client's current self-structure permits both therapist and client more adequately to consider the possible impact that any alterations in its sedimentations and dissociations will have upon the structure as a whole.

Taken together, the various shifts in the psychotherapeutic enterprise provide a viable alternative to the notion of the unconscious in that they comply with all the clinical observations associated with theories of the unconscious; they accommodate to the experimental data provided by both critics and adherents of theories concerning the unconscious; they remove the logical inconsistencies and circularities associated with theories of the unconscious; they eliminate the necessity of imposing a second hypothetical mental system over and above that of consciousness; they allow for a more parsimonious, scientifically adequate, economic and non-deterministic account of psychic conflict; and they return the focus of attention upon conscious experience as accessed and interpreted by the client.

I began this chapter by reminding readers of Freud's famous challenge to those who would attempt to refute his hypothesis of the unconscious. I leave it to them to decide whether the alternatives I have proposed succeed in providing a suitable rebuttal to that challenge.

5 Reconfiguring human sexuality

Of all the sociopolitical and interpersonal arenas in our current cultural thought upon which psychotherapeutic theories have had their impact none has been more radically affected than the terrain of human sexuality. The means by which we understand and define ourselves as sexual beings, the assumptions and expectations we hold regarding the enactment and outcome of sexual relations, the everyday concerns and most distressing fears we contemplate and consider (with more than enough assistance from every facet of our media), the way we make sense of sexual innuendo and allusion, all these – and so many more – seemingly 'natural' ways of being sexual beings can be seen to have their roots in, and continue to be reinforced by, a psychotherapeutic undercurrent.

Like it or not, aware of it or not, psychotherapeutically loaded sexual questions obsess us: Why are we attracted, or unattracted, to representatives (specific and/or general) of the opposite gender? Or of the same gender? Or of both? Or of neither? What are normal and what are perverse expressions of sexuality? Why do we fantasize sexual scenarios which we would never wish to occur in real life? How is it that incidents of sexual distress and abuse during one's childhood can provoke a wide range of (non-sexual) nervous symptoms? Or can be seemingly 'forgotten' until some sort of adult trauma (perhaps psychotherapy itself) returns them to our awareness? Or can inhibit adult expressions of sexual arousal and pleasure? Or, alternatively, can uninhibit us to the extent that we might define ourselves as being 'addicted' to sex? Or, worst of all, might lead us to re-create our trauma from the other's perspective such that we, ourselves, become sexual predators and abusers? And how is it that, in thinking about sex, we do not think of it so much in terms of what we do (or don't do) but, rather, of who we are (or are not)? The manner by which we both formulate and attempt to respond to such questions as well as the satisfaction (or lack of it) that we experience when assessing the answers provided betrays the pervasive influence of psychotherapeutic thought in general and of psychoanalytically inspired perspectives in particular.

As with many others, I hold serious reservations about the way of being with ourselves as sexual beings that is both promoted and implied by the great majority of psychotherapeutic theories. My aim, throughout this chapter, will not be anything so grandiose, or foolhardy, as the proposal of a fully developed alternative. Instead, I will focus upon three critical assumptions that infuse most psychotherapists' (and their clients') current ways of thinking about human sexuality. I will then put forward some objections and alternatives to these assumptions and consider what impact these challenges might have upon the ways in which we orient ourselves sexually in our lived relations.

While it may be odd and counter-intuitive to public consensus for us to think so, our Victorian ancestors appear to have *invented* rather than *suppressed* sexuality, insofar as their innovations set the template for our current beliefs and assumptions surrounding its defining structural characteristics. Alas, through these also emerged those apparently irresolvable issues and dilemmas that persist in troubling us, their descendants.

Even our terminology is far more recent than many of us suppose. The word 'sexuality', for instance, did not appear in English dictionaries until 1800. In similar fashion, terms such as *sex life*, *sex appeal*, and *sexy* were inventions of the first quarter of the twentieth century.[1]

Michel Foucault, in his uncompleted project *History of Sexuality*, has argued that the Victorian invention of sexuality evolved through the recognition on the part of the then relatively new bourgeoisie that its recently acquired power base was already under threat from two 'whirlwinds' of sociopolitical emancipation: the rise of the working class and the first women's liberation movement. In turn, this awareness provoked a number of attempts to control these unruly forces via various decrees; the aims of which were to institutionalize several strands of social behaviour. With regard to sexuality, such decrees were expressed via the promulgation of numerous pamphlets and learned texts preoccupied with the issues of policing the population, the maximization of its health, and the development of a new technology of control over the body. In all cases, the underlying purpose was that of *normalizing* sexuality via the pronouncement of what were its appropriate (and, more significantly, its inappropriate) expressions and practices.[2]

If one examines the literature and journalistic media of the time, one finds an explosion of exposés the concerns of which are all too similar to those we read about and discuss today: incest, birth control, divorce, prostitution, homosexuality, and sexual deviance or perversion. Further, just as is the case today, who better to pronounce upon such matters than (predominantly) men of science, and of medicine? Indeed, a new science was invented – *sexology* – whose experts (almost exclusively male medical doctors) approached the study of human sexuality via the examination of diseases, illnesses and cures associated with sexual behaviour as well as with the distinction of normal and abnormal sexual practices, desires, thoughts and cravings; and, when such 'diseases' did not seem plentiful enough, new ones could always be invented. One example of this latter tendency can be seen in the 'discovery' of a pernicious disease labelled *spermatorrhoea*.

The symptoms of spermatorrhoea were said to include

breathlessness, anxiety, bad digestion, brain fevers, epilepsy, insanity, paralysis and death, but what *was* spermatorrhoea? According to its 'discoverer', Dr John Laws Milton, spermator-rhoea is the disease of 'involuntary nocturnal seminal emis-sions'.[3] Phrased in a slightly different manner, we could say that it is 'the wet dream become waking nightmare'.

As to its remedy, Laws Milton suggests the application of cold water upon the male genitals, sleeping on the floor, military service, and, perhaps more attractive to some, the consumption of no less than a bottle of claret a day. Alterna-tively, and more extremely, he advocates the cauterization of penile skin tissue and the donning of two specially designed preventive appliances: the 'urethral ring' (a spiked circular piece of metal designed to pierce the tumescent penis), or the 'electric alarum' which administers an electric shock to the penis at the moment of erection.[4]

While all this may strike us as being risible, let me sound a word of caution. For, no matter that the disease is pure fiction, Laws Milton – and those who believed in his quackery – went on to make the claim that there existed both 'natural' and 'unnatural' types of emissions. Of the former, there was but one kind: emission through the 'connexion' resulting from heterosexual genital intercourse. All other forms of emission were deemed 'unnatural' and, hence, both leading to, and indicative of, disease.

The early sexologists took their principal arena of investi-gation to be the medico-forensic study of abnormal sexuality. In this way, they claimed, through the delineation of the unnatural and pathological practices of sexuality, they would be able to discern that which was 'natural' sexual behaviour. Hence, the plethora of sexological studies by still well-known researchers such as Richard von Krafft-Ebing, Albert Moll and Havelock Ellis typically emphasize the study of the 'unnatural' and perverse in order to pronounce upon the 'natural' and normal.[5] Equally, the language employed by such authors is cloaked in scientific medical terminology centred upon 'enlightened' notions of health and the prevention of disease rather than upon more questionable edicts derived from Judaeo–Christian doctrine – although it is remarkable how closely the former conform to the latter. Further, it should be noted that all sexological accounts assumed that the basis of sexuality lay in *biology* and ascribed a direct and seemingly unquestionable line of connection between reproduction and sexuality. Finally, the Victorian sexual revolution proposed an indissoluble link between sexual preferences and practices and the psychological issues of personality and identity such that deviant and perverse sexual practices were distinguished as aspects of, or causal antecedents to, 'sick' or perverted 'minds' or identities.

All of these revolutionary ideas continue to dominate contemporary Western views on sexuality. As such, it is to these three crucial assumptions – the link between sexuality and biology (and reproduction in particular), the contrast between 'normal' and 'perverted' sexual practices, and the connection between sexual expression and identity – upon which this chapter will focus.

First, it is important to clarify that all the early psychoanalytic views on human sexuality (as well as the overwhelming majority of its most recent reformulations) *exemplify* these very same Victorian biases and assumptions, and, through the lasting impact of psychoanalysis upon contemporary psychotherapy, these predilections remain virtually intact. Indeed, Sigmund Freud, while arguably among the more liberal of his sexological peers, nevertheless emerges as the Victorian sexologist *par excellence* since he placed sexuality firmly within the domain of biology, viewed the so-called 'sexual perversions' as deviations from either the 'natural' sexual object or the 'natural' sexual aim, and, through his constantly revised hypotheses concerning psychosexual development, proposed an indissoluble link between the 'blocks' or 'arrests' both in the development of sexual behaviour and of personality and character. Once again, while the instinct-based focus of these viewpoints and perspectives has tended to give way to more relationally derived derivations of psychoanalytic theory, the continuing assumption of some sort of 'arrest in', or deviation from, what is presumed to be normal development remains as pivotal as ever. As such, far from providing us with a radical alternative to Victorian views about human sexuality, psycho-analytic theory reveals itself to be the principal and longest lasting proponent of such views.

Let me now turn to the first of these assumptions: that human sexuality must be placed within the context of biology in general, and human reproduction in particular. This stance might at first appear as being so true and obvious that it would seem absurd for anyone to contest it. Yet, upon more careful consideration, it is evident that, unlike virtually every other creature, our desire to engage in sexual activities is not solely, nor even primarily, dictated by biological 'cycles' linked to the reproduction of the species. We do not engage in sexual relations with the principal aim that such relations will lead to the birth of our offspring. Rather, our most common sexual activities seek to ensure that just such an outcome is avoided. Indeed, *pace* Pope John Paul II, even most practising Roman Catholics seek to find ways to evade this very consequence by abstaining from penile–vaginal penetrative intercourse during 'unsafe' periods.

In addition, as indicated by the statements of those couples who, as part of either formal or informal infertility treatments, have had to engage in sexual intercourse 'on demand' in order to take the most advantage of various conditions conducive to fertilization, there exist myriad and significant experientially felt differences between these experiences and those wherein procreation was neither the principal, nor sought after, intent. The desire to 'make love' is not the same as the desire to 'make babies'. Nor are the felt experiences associated with each the same. While there may be a biological imperative with regard to the latter, I would seriously question the assumption that such an imperative fuels the former.

The person who has highlighted this distinction most clearly is the French existential phenomenologist Maurice Merleau-Ponty.[6] In his illuminating discussion on the body, Merleau-Ponty argued that the body is not a 'thing' among other 'things' to which one's consciousness is somehow affiliated. Rather, ours is an *embodied consciousness*. Our body is '*the vehicle of being-in-the-world and a basic form of the appearance (manifestation) of the world itself*'.[7] It is the configuration through which all of our existential projects are realized. That is to say, our body expresses our unique dialogue with the world.

Merleau-Ponty stresses the intersubjective quality of incarnational consciousness such that each of us interprets the world through our body and, in parallel, interprets our body through the world. In summarizing this view, George Kovacs notes:

> **The body is not just a means or a secondary instrument of human existence in the world, but the very expression of existence . . . My body expresses my existence in all its facticity and aliveness. For instance, by shaking hands my entire body (not only my hand) expresses (on many levels) the type of welcome (hesitant, happy, fearful, nauseating) my presence (existence) grants to the appearance of another human being.[8]**

This last point provides us with the necessary indication as to Merleau-Ponty's existential-phenomenological analysis of human sexuality. Sexual encounters provide us with a pivotal means with which to express our presence to 'the other' and, in turn, to express the presence of 'the other' to ourselves. Merleau-Ponty is not interested in the issues of male or female sexuality, sexual orientation or the sociopolitical dimensions of sexuality. His is an investigation aimed towards the clarification of sexuality *as it is revealed in its interrelational dimensions.*

The importance of sexuality for Merleau-Ponty lies in its ability to 'awaken' each of us to our interrelational being. His stance presents us with a conception of sexuality that expresses a world-view in its totality – and not just a limited expression of 'genitality'.

It seems to me that if we follow through with this line of argument, we are presented with a view of sexuality that undermines all assumptions regarding its links to any biological imperatives derived from reproductive drives. Instead, it places sexuality firmly within the arena of the interrelational and posits that it is a sublime expression of each being's active desire to establish a presence through which he or she can engage with, and be engaged by, others and the world in general – even if the focus of such engagements rests upon the denial of others' presence and impact or demands the creation of imaginary others who pose no threat to us and who conform to our every demand and desire. How we are sexually, and what we enact sexually, therefore become not statements of reproductive drive but, rather, expressive stratagems of our choices, hesitations, delights and anxieties in exploring the *being-with* of self and other through a body, or incarnational, dialogue.

The implications of this view for psychotherapy are, I think, obvious and significant. For most, the problem with sex lies in its wider interrelational expressions. Just as presenting sexual issues whose initial focus lies in physiological dysfunctions will most commonly reveal more broad-based concerns dealing with any number of social interactions with one's sexual partner (or other persons in general), so, too, may issues like the experience of lack of trust in oneself or another, or a sensed loss of direction in a relationship, or the unwillingness or inability to form intimate relationships, express themselves in an embodied manner through the whole, or specific parts, of the body – including, not surprisingly, those parts of the body associated with sexual expression. Whatever the means of expression, it reveals the range of possibilities and limits (whether plentiful or restricted) through which each of us discloses who and how he or she is willing to be with self and other. As Hans W. Cohn points out:

> Problems can arise when clients feel that a desired sexual activity becomes difficult or impossible. Clients may feel that masturbation takes the place of sexual relations with others, or that orgasm is dependent upon wearing certain kinds of clothes. Such activities become problematic for clients because they feel they are 'not normal' by the rules of their sociocultural context – even though they are quite happy with the way they experience sexual satisfaction. But it can also be that they would prefer a different way of sexual activity which appears to them more meaningful . . . The important point is that it is they who are not satisfied, and not the therapist who judges them to be 'immature' or 'inadequate' and in need of being 'sorted out'.[9]

Just as obviously, this stance frees us from the need to explain all the varied manifestations of sexuality in a fashion that must ultimately reduce them to their bio-reproductive origins.

Let me explain this view via a simplistic analogy. According to the ideas being proposed, there would be a significant divergence of both meaning and intent when contrasting the experience of eating in order to provide physical nourishment and eating with friends in a restaurant. While both situations may, in some instances, allow both physical and interrelational nourishment, it is evident that both may also be kept separate. My body may not require any intake of food and drink in the latter situation, but such activities may be vital components of my ability and willingness to be with others in ways that are mutually interrelationally satisfying. In similar fashion, no amount of solitary intake of food and drink will satisfy my experienced *hunger*, or sense of *emptiness* in my intersubjective relations. Once again, such views may be of value to our understanding and treatment of various eating disorders.

Human sexuality is greatly impoverished if it is surmised either solely or principally from the standpoint of bio-reproductive imperatives. But consider how much more pertinent and revealing its exploration becomes when 'being sexual' is viewed as an expression of interrelational disclosure – regardless of how limited or fulfilling the experience might be in any given encounter. Similarly, instead of requiring the necessity of reducing all other forms of engagement with the world as displaced, sublimated or symbolic expressions of overarching libidinal drives or of tensions arising from arrests in the development of mature object relations, this alternative focus 'stays with' and examines the embodied meanings that structure our way of being in the manner by which they are revealed (as they are). With this alternative perspective in mind, I can now begin to consider the second area of enquiry: the contrast of 'natural' to 'unnatural', or 'normal' to 'perverse' forms of sexual relations.

Once again, it is important to recall that both psychoanalytic theory and most psychotherapeutic theories in general embrace and demand such distinctions since they are necessary to their models' insistence upon reducing them either to their bio-reproductive drive origins, or to primitive intrapsychic object relations. If, however, we adopt the perspective inspired by Merleau-Ponty, we are forced to ask: Just what constitutes a sexual *perversion*? If we can no longer rely upon biology to guide our thinking as to what may be normal or abnormal, natural or unnatural sexual expression, we have no universally predetermined basis upon which to make our pronouncements. Instead, all that we have available to us is something far more tenuous, and far more revealing of our individual and sociocultural biases and assumptions. Allow me to provide a hopefully amusing example in order to clarify this argument.

I am lying in bed, my bare back turned away from my wife. I experience a sensation that I interpret as that of my wife licking the space between my shoulders. Remaining in my position, I say to her that I am enjoying these sensations and encourage her to continue. In response, my wife replies that, if so, I should be thanking our cat, Siggy, since it is he who is doing the licking. I immediately jump up, suddenly disturbed, and emit a loud 'Euchh!' that expresses not only my sudden displeasure but also an implicit assumption that it is somehow 'perverse' of me to allow myself to be 'turned on' by a cat. At this, my wife laughs, informs me that she was joking, and that it has been she who all along had been licking my back. Immediately, the seeming 'perversity' of the experience and its accompanying sense of displeasure dissipate, and I allow myself to reinterpret the experience as both enjoyable and acceptable.

What is evident here is that the same stimulus provoked radically differing reactions. As such, it was not the act itself, but my *interpretations* of the act – such as who was administering it and what I allowed as 'proper' instances of arousal – that were the decisive factors.

A similar instance can be seen in the Neil Jordan film *The Crying Game*,[10] wherein the principal character who has previously enjoyed the experience of being fellated by the female nightclub singer whom he has recently met suddenly discovers that 'she' is most definitely a 'he', and immediately becomes violently ill.

Both these examples raise interesting questions – some of which I will return to in the final section of this chapter. For now, all that needs be said is that our experience of, and ability to designate, the perverse, is no straightforward matter and, rather than point us towards biology, our attempts direct us squarely to the much more relative realm of interpersonal and sociocultural biases.

If it is a verity that all cultures designate what is both a natural and a perverse expression of sexuality, it is equally true that wide areas of disagreement exist as to which activities are so labelled. Further, it is also the case that what the same culture views as perverse at one point in time can, and does, alter at another. For example, only about thirty years ago, most North Americans viewed all oral–genital acts between consenting adults to be perverse, to the extent that, in some states, these activities were designated as being criminal and could lead to fines or imprisonment.[11] Today, these same acts, at least insofar as they are between heterosexual partners, are taken to be both acceptable and desirable. In contrast, in Britain at present, while anal intercourse between homosexual partners past the age of consent is a legal activity, the same behaviour between heterosexual partners remains illegal. More generally, and far more disturbingly, it is important to recall that only fifty years ago, in various European countries, young, unmarried women who engaged in sexual relations with several male partners were, if discovered, labelled 'mad' and subsequently incarcerated and, to put it bluntly, tortured by their psychiatrists via the use of electro-convulsive therapy and lobotomy (or leucotomy). Once again, the basis for such decisions was derived from highly dubious biological theories.

If we have progressed in our attitudes, such progressions reveal only that we have reinterpreted in a more open and accepting fashion that which we label as 'normal' and 'perverse'. However, if our histories teach us anything it is that we must remain cautious in our positive evaluations of ourselves. What we take to be either normal or perverse today undoubtedly remains open to future re-evaluation.

In our own culture's case, our persistently negative dominant attitudes towards any form of homosexual relations should serve to remind us of how suppressive our views remain. Homosexual relations still stand out, for most members of our culture, as the primary expression of, at best inadequate, at worst pathological and perverse forms of sexual expression. But, here, too, one should note that such labels only make sense, and retain their emotive and explanatory power, when placed within the context of bio-reproductive assumptions regarding human sexuality. Once again, such activities can only be labelled as 'unnatural' if contextualized within reductive assumptions of 'reproductively directed sexual impulses that have gone awry'. Once this assumption is questioned, and dismissed as being inadequate, what we are left with is the obvious: that rather than express some form of pathology, be it the result of biochemistry, genetics or, as Freud suggested, *'a variation of a sexual function produced by a certain arrest of sexual development,'*[12] homosexual relations express the very same interrelational stances regarding one's relative willingness or unwillingness to be with others as can be ascertained in all other sexual manifestations.

That these may be the chosen means by which an individual both expresses and avoids interrelational anxieties, that they may both allow and prevent particular forms of self/other dialogue, that they may be dependent upon interpretational distinctions as to what form of dialogue is acceptable or desirable with reference to particular categories of 'others', reveals nothing that is not similarly revealed in any other form of sexual relation, such that to distinguish this particular means of disclosure as inherently different, unique, problematic or perverse has no basis – other than at the level of an interpretative bias that must be challenged rather than condoned. However, any such attempted challenge reveals significant problems. Perhaps the most trenchant among these emerges with the recognition that an increasingly significant proportion of men and women who have been labelled, and who label themselves, as homosexual have come to accept and promulgate those 'biologically essentialist' views that single them out as different, unique, problematic and, indeed, perverse.

The search for a broadly biological basis for homosexuality has, if anything, increased since the days of the pioneer sexologists. Neuro-endocrinal explanations,[13] have given way to hypothalamic and morphological solutions[14] and, even more recently, to genetic factors found in the Xq28 region of the X chromosome.[15] Needless to say, all such findings raise more problems than offer solutions.

Speaking personally, I find the acceptance of these studies by anyone espousing broadly 'liberationist' or 'progressive' views as being deeply disturbing. It may be true that these appear to provide the means by which an individual is no longer held accountable or responsible for being the way he or she is sexually, since such is the result of a biologically derived anomaly that, in being so viewed, allows some gains regarding matters of employment, personal insurance and the like. Nevertheless, the price of accepting such is nothing less than the admission of an inherent difference, deficiency and/or abnormality in one's very being. Perhaps the continual heterosexually inspired oppression of, and antagonism towards, those labelled 'homosexual' may have served to make such separatist options seem substantially preferable to previous alternatives. Certainly, similar stances have been adopted by sizeable numbers of other harassed and persecuted groups. Acknowledging this, and acknowledging as well that I speak as one who has suffered little by way of harassment and persecution, I remain distrustful of such isolationist perspectives – not least because they both validate and maintain the employment of labels such as 'abnormal' and 'perverse'.

Is there an alternative? I think there is and, as must be acknowledged, its basis lies in a decidedly Freudian pronouncement. In a footnote to the 1915 edition of *Three Essays on the Theory of Sexuality*,[16] Freud posited that '*from the point of view of psychoanalysis the exclusive sexual interest felt by men for women is also a problem that needs elucidating'.*[17] In other words, in response to the question 'Why homosexuality?' Freud asks, quite correctly, 'Why *exclusive* heterosexuality?' I emphasize the word 'exclusive' since this implicit qualification is of central importance to Freud's argument, even if it has passed by most other commentators. Freud could not truly ask 'Why heterosexuality?' since this query would dismantle the whole of his bio-reproductive model of sexuality. All he could ask was 'Why not, sometimes, both?' The limitations of his own model could not allow him to ask the more pertinent and revolutionary question.

However, since this chapter seeks to provide alternatives to psychoanalytic assumptions, there is nothing to prevent the asking of that same question as openly as possible. In so doing, I move to the last of the major concerns: the relation between sexuality and identity.

As a starting point, a pertinent quote by Michel Foucault is worth repeating:

> **Homosexuality appeared as one of the forms of sexuality when it was transposed from the practice of sodomy into a kind of interior androgyny, a hermaphrodism of the soul. The sodomite had been a temporary aberration; the homosexual was now a species.**[18]

Considered more generally, Foucault's observation reminds us that the behaviour under question has existed in all societies since the dawn of our species. What is new is that the activity has become a principal means by which to identify a particular way of 'being sexual' that extends far beyond the boundaries of the activity itself. Such a development allows a crucial internalization to occur: *The act has become a person.* Now, all of us are able to identify ourselves either as 'beings who are

– or are not – the activity'. In other words, what we do, or do not do, has become who we are, or are not.

Among a number of authors who have explored this point, both the sexologist Alfred Kinsey[19] and the novelist and essayist Gore Vidal[20] have argued that the word 'homosexual' should only be used as an adjective to describe sexual activity and not as a noun to describe and identify a particular type of being. In this, they echo Foucault's warning that the Western compulsion to categorize sexual acts leads inevitably to the construction of sexual categories of identity. Foucault suggests that the way in which we structure our thoughts changes the thoughts themselves. As an extension of this view, I would remind readers of the arguments presented in Chapters 3 and 4 and suggest that the self-structure imposes limits that force us to both sediment and dissociate various experiences of being-in-the-world – including, of course, sexual experiences.

It is vital to note that just as such consequences are applicable to the correlation of homosexual acts with the construction of a 'homosexual identity', so, too, is it the case that the correlation of heterosexual acts (or, indeed, *any* sexual act) with the construction of a 'heterosexual identity' (or a 'sexual identity' in general) imposes significant sedimentations and dissociations regarding our experience of interrelational being. Once again, it becomes apparent that it is not the activities in themselves, but rather the particular personal and socio-cultural *meanings* associated with them that are of importance to the current debate on human sexuality.

Terms such as *homosexual* and *heterosexual* serve as structured meaning instruments of self-definition. Indeed, with regard to these particular terms, it is evident that each requires the other in order to provide itself with any substantial meaning. It is equally apparent that such labels as *straight*, *gay* or *queer* now extend far beyond the specific confines of sexual preferences in that they allude to, or are identified by many, as compacted statements regarding sociopolitical attitudes and affiliations, economic classifications, and personal and group empowerment. However, it must be asked: How valid are these demarcations of identity?

On reflection, I would suggest, they enforce an insidious form of separationist stereotyping that has little basis in the lived reality and identity of most of us. The labels *heterosexual* or *homosexual*, while alluding to some unified meaning, instead reveal a wide range of differing and competing meanings. One might label oneself as *heterosexual* or *homosexual* in order to express one's preferred, or most personally satisfactory, means of achieving sexual pleasure and comfort. Indeed, they may express the *only* means to have been found, or desired, through which to be sexual. But yet . . . Someone else may identify with such labels in order to express his or her comfort or discomfort with traditional gender roles. For another, the adoption of either term is not intended to imply that his or her sexual relations need remain exclusively associated with the same or opposite gender, and that, indeed, sexual relations with the same or the opposite gender are experienced as being pleasurable and meaningful even if the pleasure and meaning given them might be labelled as 'different'. And still another who might identify with either label might do so without wishing to suggest that he or she engages in *any* form of sexual relations with the same or opposite gender. Someone else may adopt such labels so as to express a stance of personal and social rebellion or compliance. And for yet another, these labels make sense as expressions of a yearning for a parent 'who never was' or one who remains 'ever present'.

Acknowledging all of the above, and not wishing to suggest criticism of any, none the less the overwhelming evidence pointing to the potential plasticity inherent in all of these definitions and redefinitions, whatever their sexual direction, reveals that, far from being 'fixed' in biology, our sexual identities rely much more upon constructivist variables. Social and personal changes in circumstance do lead at least some individuals (whose prior ways of being sexual were fixed (sedimented), clear, secure and satisfactory to them) to reassess their interpretative stance towards any or all of these variables, and, in turn, to redefine (to de-sediment and re-sediment) their sexual self-structure. In some cases, these reassessments and re-identifications can occur several times throughout an individual's life. In other instances, the strength of dissociation of experience required to maintain a particularly rigid sedimentation of the self-structure will not permit any sexual realignment regardless of even the most radical social or cultural changes or alternatives in the individual's personal circumstances.

All the above points raise significant concerns; but if the association of sexual stances with personal identity remains problematic, not least because of the inconsistencies and limitations that this link imposes, what allows it to persist for all of us? Kenneth Plummer provides a concise and valid explanation that also serves as a restatement of the broader notion of sedimentations and dissociations of the self-structure: '*With all these categorisations comes the paradox: they control, restrict and inhibit whilst simultaneously providing comfort, security and assurances*'.[21]

Here, I think, lies the crux of the issue. In associating sexual attitudes and behaviours with sexual identity, we impose a fixedness in our 'sexual way-of being' whose value lies precisely in the *identificatory security* (however limiting and problematic) that it provides.

As an extreme version of this, our culture's current obsession with representations of sexuality as 'a product' whose worth and value can be weighed and measured in the most obvious and superficial of ways reflects an increasing tendency to identify one's 'self' through such things as the designer clothes one wears or the labelled products one owns and displays. In turn, this tendency might well be shown to express the emphasis we place upon immediate, if superficial, communication signifiers and 'sound-bites' – designed to advertise and make desirable anything at all – not least our sexual interests and lifestyle. While these may seem to be initially attractive options, the ever-increasing sense of ennui and alienation that this strategy also evokes is beginning to become apparent.

Why then are we, or why do we become, 'sexual' in the ways that we are? There exists no real answer to this. One could equally ask: 'Why do I prefer one colour to another?' or 'Why do I write/not-write books?' In spite of our assumptions that answers to such questions rely upon past experiences (whether remembered or repressed, in whole or part), a more adequate, if disquieting alternative is provided by existential theory. This view argues that 'the past' as evoked at any moment in time, cannot be isolated from the evoking being's current (or present) meaning constructs, as well as that being's future-directed intentions. With this shift in perspective, the past can be seen to be not the causal determinant of our current self-structure, but rather as a *'highly selective interpretative construct designed to validate, or to provide evidence for, a being's current sedimented self-structure'*.[22] In other words, the past that we recall allows us to maintain the self we believe we are, or must be, through the very 'invention' or construction of 'critical moments' that have 'made us the way we are'.

This view would suggest that we identify ourselves as homosexual, heterosexual or any-kind-of-sexual not because of past circumstances, or biological dictates, but because *it is who we say – or insist – we are*. And, in saying so, we provide the current self-structure, whether it be focused upon our more general ways of being or the more specific ways we adopt of 'being sexual', with its meaning and validity.

As Jean-Paul Sartre so succinctly put it: 'We are our choices'.[23]

6 Conflicting desires: childhood and sexuality

It is, I believe, an indication of the times in which we currently live that I find it necessary to begin this chapter with a point of clarification. While the discussion that follows raises what I imagine to be some relevant concerns regarding the issue of children and sexuality, I want to make it absolutely clear to all readers that none of my comments should be understood to be either an overt or subtle defence of child pornography or paedophilia. I remain as aware as any of my psychotherapeutic colleagues of the long-term physical and psychological injuries that can be inflicted upon those people who, as young children, suffered the unwanted and undeserved attentions of sexual predators – be they strangers or, far more commonly, family members. And, like my colleagues, I have no hesitation in expressing my revulsion at the behaviour of those who, for whatever reasons, construct the means with which to permit themselves the enactment and enjoyment of sexual violence towards children – no matter how seemingly affectionate, tender or focused upon the 'pleasuring' of the child they claim these acts to be. If my arguments succeed in presenting readers with reflections that promote a sense of unease, it should become equally apparent that this felt discomfort is not one that is intended to exculpate moral responsibilities.

The great majority of contemporary psychotherapists subscribe to the notion that the means through which adults structure their sexual habits and preferences originate, at least in significant part, in their earliest infantile and early childhood experiences. Usually, and incorrectly, Sigmund Freud's theories arguing that, rather than being an outcome of adolescence, we are sexual beings from birth have been presented as being the first to posit this relationship.[1] While Freud undoubtedly pioneered a radical and multi-faceted theoretical perspective on this question, it remains the case that just about every one of the individual components that make up his theory (such as pre-adolescent masturbatory activity, the stage-like progression from oral to anal to genital 'zones' of sexual focus and fixation and the child's innate bisexual (or multi-sexual) orientation) which, when considered as a whole, attempt to substantiate its hypotheses, had been topics widely discussed among sexologists whose writings either preceded or were contemporary to Freud's.[2] In similar fashion, the wider concerns surrounding the then (as now) not uncommon sexual abuse of children and its impact upon the appearance of later adult sexual dysfunctions discussed by Freud in his preliminary 'seduction hypothesis' were both noted and stressed by various concurrent texts and pamphlets written by medical doctors, clergymen and social reformers.[3] None the less, implicit in all these issues that continue to arouse our anxieties today is the underlying assumption that the conjunction of the terms *childhood* and *sexuality* is a problematic one. But what makes it so?

As an initial response, one might suggest, if not insist, that children differ from adults in a great many ways – physically, mentally, emotionally, relationally – and must be permitted to develop towards maturity without being subject to unnecessary or retarding demands imposed by adults. Of these, the adult's claim to sexual services is viewed as being the most likely to not only hamper the child's development but also remain as a considerable encumbrance upon any subsequent adult relations. As an extension of this argument, childhood is commonly perceived as being not only different, but 'special' and 'innocent'. The introduction of sexuality would seem to threaten the maintenance of these qualities. As such, if we must concede that young children are sexual beings, their sexuality must be of a different 'kind' to that of adults, for it must also retain qualities of 'specialness' and 'innocence'. So prevalent is this set of assumptions in our current society that it appears odd to us to consider the possibility of any alternatives to it. Yet, alternatives have existed both in the history of our culture and in the more specific historical development of our current notions of childhood.[4]

As various authors have pointed out, childhood as we understand the term to mean today is a relatively recent invention whose origins lie in the social and religious upheavals of the seventeenth century. For several centuries prior to these events, children were likely to have been perceived as being 'miniature adults' who shared similar duties, responsibilities, interests and passions with their 'full-sized' counterparts. These 'miniature adults' worked long hours, dressed in the same (if smaller-sized) clothes, ate the same food and participated in the same gatherings and festivities as did the other members of their community. To have segregated them would likely have been viewed as being cruel and unjust. Equally, under such conditions, these 'miniature adults' must surely have also witnessed, if not participated in, various forms of sexual activity that, today, would be viewed as being entirely unacceptable, if not perverse, for children to be aware of, much less engage in either with other children or adults.[5]

Our cultural shift in perspective came about largely as a result of the Reformation and Counter-Reformation movements. Through these, the view was promulgated that children's souls were purer, expressive of a more innocent state of being, if only because by merit of their being younger, children had had far fewer experiences of 'the baser instincts' directed towards violence and sexuality than had had either their adult or older companions. With these new religious ideas came various attempts to protect the child (and the child's soul, in particular) from exposure to impure thoughts and deeds, for to be exposed to such would surely lead to their imitative enactment by the child and this, in turn, would stain the soul with sin.

The segregation of children from the world of the adult was one obvious safeguarding manoeuvre. The attempt to educate at least some children so that the influence both of religious faith and an appreciation of 'higher' intellectual qualities which could counteract their more 'animalistic' tendencies and urges was another. The wearing of particular clothing, different to that of the adult, in order to highlight and distinguish the child from the adult and thereby serve as a signpost and reminder that the latter should apply a different code of conduct towards all relations with the former was yet another means by which the child's relative spiritual purity and state of grace could be prolonged. In similar fashion, any evidence of the young child's curiosity surrounding the body and its functions – and particularly its sexual and reproductive functions – or, worse, of the child's indulging in activities such as solitary or mutual masturbation, required swift and unequivocal controls (usually through acts of physical punishment combined with the production of fear focused upon the wrath of God) for the sake of protecting the child's soul and mind from malign sinful influences leading to premature and irreparable spiritual and mental degeneration.

In appreciating these huge cultural shifts in perspective, we can begin to see how these influences have endured, at least in part, such that they continue to inform and dominate contemporary views of childhood and, in turn, how they infuse and identify our deepest recurring fears for and about our children. Indeed, today, as has been made obvious by the groundswell of community vigilantism focused upon the forced eviction from their homes of convicted paedophiles who have served their prison sentence, the highest levels of parental dread continue to be aroused by issues arising from the interface between childhood and sexuality.

Just as pertinently, we can better comprehend just how disturbing and radical were the 'new' ideas about infantile sexuality being proposed by Freud and his contemporaries and why they generated so much heated debate and disapproval. For, in order to accept the validity of these views, what was required was a fundamental shift not only in how to redefine childhood but, just as significantly, how to redefine the parameters of proper engagement between children and adults at every level of interaction – including, of course, expressions of sexuality.

When we consider our current attitudes and expectations regarding children, what becomes apparent is that while we have accepted many of the assumptions and hypotheses provoked by the Freudian revolution, we also still cling to notions that are more aligned with a pre-Freudian perspective. The issue of sexuality makes this confusion all too apparent. On the one hand, we tend to concede that children are *sexual* to some degree while at the same time we wish to imbue them with some sort of state of sexual innocence. It is possible that this confusion of ideas may, at the very least, exacerbate our fears and concerns.

To be fair, Freud posited early childhood sexuality to be different from that of the adult in that early expressions of sexuality have no focused object. This *polymorphous perversity* permits any part of the infant's body, as well as any perceived external object, to become 'libidinally charged' such that it can become the means to auto-erotic sexual gratification. It is only when the proper object-choice (typically, the child's mother) is identified as the external satisfier of the child's sexual aim that the child begins to approach a relationship with sexuality that shares primary characteristics with that of adult expressions of sexuality.[6]

This basic hypothesis underwent numerous revisions by Freud himself. Even so, he continued to accept its fundamental accuracy. Others, especially those psychoanalysts who never entered Freud's 'inner circle', posited even more radical elaborations. Melanie Klein, for example, took Freud's ideas to the extreme by arguing that, among other notions, the psychic world of the young infant is best understood as seething with sexual desires that are often expressed through the child's play activity. This activity, when properly interpreted, reveals the child's preoccupation with attempts both to incorporate and destroy the play-object. Through such observations, Klein hypothesized the existence of an innate infantile phantasy of male and female genitalia bound together in permanent intercourse. As such, unlike Freud's vision of a childhood sexuality that must undergo various phases before it reaches its genital focus, Klein considered this focus to be all too apparent from birth – if the adult dared witness it.[7]

In complete contrast to this line of enquiry, Freud's once most likely successor and subsequently the most significant of his detractors, Carl Gustav Jung, dismissed the whole idea of a pre-adolescent sexuality. Jung argued that the language of psychoanalysis is that of adult sexual experience imposing itself upon and interpreting certain childhood behaviours such that these become 'sexualized'. According to Jung, the adult interprets some of the child's actions as being primarily, or even solely, sexual not because the child experiences them directly as such but rather because sexual meanings are imposed upon the child's behaviour by the adult whose biased way of observing the behaviour and whose interpretative language of it is structured and bounded by adult sexual experience.[8]

Jung's argument is, I think, a powerful one and is certainly deserving of much greater consideration by psychotherapists. In many ways, it foreshadows perspectives presented in Chapter 5 where it was suggested that it would be worthwhile to consider expressions of sexuality as being principally interrelational constructs rather than innate biologically driven behaviours. None the less, it might still be argued that even if

Jung's theory is substantially correct, it might still be the case that the adult's 'sexualizing' interpretations of the child's actions could conceivably still accurately reflect the child's own lived sexuality. In other words, that the child cannot label the experience as *sexual* need not imply that it is not 'felt' sexually. In this way, Jung's hypothesis shares intriguing similarities with Freud's own early, and subsequently discarded, 'seduction hypothesis' wherein he argues that those repressed pre-adolescent experiences of sexual abuse become 'unrepressed' at adolescence because, by then, a language has been found to express and bring meaning to the earlier experience.

This diversity of viewpoints continues to dominate our thinking about the relationship between childhood and sexuality. However, as has perhaps begun to become apparent, in part, at least, the crux of the problem lies in the term *sexual*. What is implied by it? Are adults and children *sexual* in similar or differing ways?

Acknowledging the unreliability of memory and that we review our remembrances from the biased perspective of the present, I suspect that most of us could single out events from our childhood which we would categorize as being *sexual*. I remember, for instance, that as a young child, I was an active participant in any number of secretive games with other children whose principal purpose was the revealing and fondling of one another's genitals. As well as this 'fact', I can also recall the general excitement felt when engaging in such games and the more localized pleasurable physical throbbing of my penis when it was being touched and fondled by my playmates. Further, when I consider these sensations in relation to those experienced by me in adolescent and adult sexual situations, their similarities far outweigh their differences. Similarly, I can recall night-time childhood fantasies that I conjured up for myself just before falling asleep. Most of these involved television characters (such as, I am embarrassed to admit, the actors in the *I Love Lucy* comedies) stripping off their clothes and fondling one another's genitals. Again, are such fantasies *so* different from the private masturbatory rituals of adolescents and adults? And is the experience of physical pleasure derived from the former significantly dissimilar to that gained from the latter?

As was previously suggested, one possible, and important, difference might well lie in the identification of an activity as being sexual. Again, while as children we might well have used words like *sex* or *sexy*, what these terms denoted was something all too mysterious and unfocused. In effect, they were 'naughty' words designed to provoke awe and laughter from our companions rather than serve as attempts to delineate the nature of our actions. Even when the delight experienced by our fondling was genitally focused, were we interpreting such feelings as specifically 'sexual' as might an adult, or were they localized focal-points contained within a much more diffuse lived experience that included elements of curiosity, shared secrecy, intimacy, humour, comparison and ritual and which, together, provoked the general experience of pleasure?

Perhaps it might be worthwhile to consider these possible differences, and their implications for the issues surrounding childhood sexuality, in the following way: physically pleasurable experiences might be distinguished as being either *arousing* or *erotic*.

Arousing experiences refer to those physical sensations that may be felt diffusely throughout the whole of one's body or that are localized upon particular parts of the body (such as the genitals), or both, and whose aim and focus lies in their maintenance of a persistent state of pleasurable body alertness and excitation that lasts until such time as the participant/s cease the activities that are required to provoke them.

Erotic experiences may share similar features with arousing experiences but are distinguishable from them in that their intent is the release of physical tension through orgasm. As such, from a felt standpoint, erotic experiences may be in part, or entirely, genitally focused.

Pleasurable experiences may be both arousing and erotic or may shift from one to the other. When these defined pleasurable experiences are enacted with one or more partners, it is possible that while one participant experiences arousal, the other(s) may be experiencing erotic excitation and vice versa, or that both (or all) experience either only arousal or erotic excitation.

While I remain aware that the terms *arousal* and *erotic* are somewhat loaded and only meaningful within the parameters of contemporary Western culture, and that *erotic* is more commonly employed within this culture to designate non-pornographic depictions of nudity and sexual activity, I hope that this limited distinction will none the less serve to address and clarify a possibly critical divergence between child and adult sexuality as perceived by contemporary Western culture. What I am suggesting is that, at least insofar as they refer to existent conditions within our culture, childhood experiences of looking at or fondling the whole or parts of one's own or another's body, or having parts or the whole of one's body fondled by another, are typically instances of arousal whereas adult experiences can be either arousing or erotic, or both.

What value might this distinction have? For one thing, it acknowledges that children may seek out arousing experiences while still remaining 'innocent' of their erotic counterpart. Further, it clarifies that while interactions between children and adults may provoke arousal for either or both participants, such experiences need not be erotic for either or both parties. Finally, it may also be the case that the cultural concerns and alarms raised by child pornography and paedophilia alert us to the distinction between arousing and erotic activities, and that while the former category may be condoned or even encouraged (and even then perhaps only when diffuse) between children and adults, the latter category is properly condemned within our current culture as being an abusive assertion of sexual demands upon another (the child) who might neither understand their meaning nor consent to their imposition by the adult.

It is possible, as well, that the proposed distinction between the arousing and the erotic may also serve to clarify the increasingly fearful confusion felt by many adults (parents in particular) with regard to their experience of physical pleasure when holding, fondling, bathing or engaging in other forms of physical contact with their offspring. Given our culture's current tendency to view the sexual abuse of children as being the one remaining great taboo and 'ultimate perversion', it is not surprising that adults who have neither the desire nor intent to sexually abuse their children might question any potentially 'abnormal' arousal feelings they may have towards their own or other people's children and arrive at shameful and life-destroying conclusions about themselves.

For instance, one of my clients, Sally, confessed to me her delight in kissing the whole of her three-month-old son's body, including his genitals, as part of their evening post-bathing ritual. She added that her own experience of these activities provoked a sense of bonding and near-spiritual closeness with her son but that, while being undoubtedly physical and arousing for her, this arousal was diffuse (in her words, 'it made the whole of her body tingle') rather than be principally, or entirely, localized upon her primary erotogenic zones. Was she, she wanted to know, a pervert? Was she sexually abusing her child? There is no easy nor straightforward answer to her question. None the less, the proposed distinction between arousal and erotic excitation could well have assisted her in arriving at an adequate resolution to her dilemma.

In similar fashion, many of the more familiar problems and difficulties encountered within adult sexual relations might be clarified and reduced through this distinction. For example, that one or both partners might not experience any specifically erotic excitement in their physical encounters need not lead us to conclude that *no* arousal is being experienced or that the arousal that might be being experienced is somehow less adequate, or less fulfilling, than its erotic counterpart. In any case, there is good reason to suppose that the proposed distinction between arousing and erotic experiences might be helpful in clarifying the contradictory assumptions we hold regarding childhood and sexuality and, as well, in addressing the legitimate fears surrounding the sexual abuse of children that we maintain. Nevertheless, a further, related set of concerns remains to be addressed.

The sexual revolution regarding our view of childhood initiated by radical thinkers such as Freud and numerous subsequent authors, while undoubtedly liberating and laudable in intent and potential, has contributed to a slow but steady return to earlier notions of children as 'miniature adults'. Children today have viewpoints, responsibilities and attitudes thrust upon them that increasingly liken them to the adult. From their own accounts, and by the reckoning of their parents and educators, today's children have taken on more adult lifestyles, concerns and anxieties that even in recent earlier generations, such as the one of which I am a member, would have been inconceivable.

One indication of this shift can be seen in the growing lack of distinction between adult and child clothing. Designer wear for children is a booming industry and, more to the point, is based upon the provision of miniature versions of adult wear. This, of itself, is nothing that should necessarily provoke unease or concern. What does raise alarm is that in the increasingly apparent consumer-focused culture we inhabit, the products we purchase and consume can be seen to serve as 'signifiers' of our identity in that how we define ourselves has become more and more focused upon material 'things'. With regard to clothing and related apparel, for instance, the brand names and designer labels we wear have begun to contribute ever more substantially to a person's sense of self-worth, value and potential, as well as to a wide variety of broader attitudinal and identity-related factors. For more and more of us, what we wear *is* who we are. While it might be the case that children have always been concerned with how they look, in recent years *how 'they look' is how adults 'look'*. If, as has been suggested, clothing serves as a (partial) signifier to an adult's sense of identity, is there not a likely possibility that children, too, have begun to take on the *adult* attitudinal and identity-related factors that have come to be associated with these products?[9]

However, this shift in perspective is not uni-directional. For, just as children have begun to adopt more adult-like stances, interests and behaviours, so, too, have adults become increasingly infantalized in terms of their relationship towards themselves, others and the world in general so that the demarcations between childhood and adulthood are becoming increasingly 'fuzzy' and indistinct from one another. Their once separate 'worlds' have begun to merge.

It has become less and less common, for instance, for children to engage in prolonged play activities solely in the company of other children of similar ages. Children's games and sports activities, television programmes and films, reading material and music, preferred food and beverages – all generate huge and ever-expanding adult involvement. From *Star Wars* to *Harry Potter*, from *Barbie Dolls* to *Playstation2*, from favourite sports team emblazoned caps and shirts to the participation in competitive activities of every kind, what was once the domain of the child and young adolescent has become infiltrated by the adult. While we might well applaud the greater willingness on the part of parents to set aside ever-increasing amounts of time and attention in the company of their young children, we must also consider the possible, if unintended, consequences of this.

Of course, children of previous generations engaged in fantasy games that centred around their playing at 'grown-ups' by dressing in their parents' clothes or focusing upon adult roles and activities. What is different today, however, is that such games are being played out by children in the presence and with the encouragement of their parents and other adults. While, in many instances, such shared activities are enjoyed by children and adults alike with no sense of possible harm or danger, taken to their extreme they present us with questionable spectacles such as television programmes that parade young children dressed up and gyrating suggestively in imitation of adult actors and singers. Again, it is not that such activities are novel behavioural expressions for children to undertake; rather it is that, increasingly, they are being enacted as much for the pleasure and titillation of adults as for that of their similarly aged peers. At the same time, this shift is further exacerbated by adults' willingness to adopt increasingly infantilizing interests, attitudes and behaviours. Just as children are once again adopting a 'miniature adult' world-view, so, too, are adults exhibiting characteristics of 'overgrown children'.

If this confusion of childhood and adulthood extends to all manner of seemingly safe territories of expression and identification, is it not worthwhile to ask whether such confusion also extends into less desirable and more worrisome domains such as that of sexuality? For, if the child is becoming increasingly similar to the adult in such wide-ranging ways, how can we state with any certainty that these similarities have not begun to include specifically sexual interests and behaviours?

In the UK today, our fears surrounding the sexual abuse of children have been substantially compounded by the apprehensive recognition that children are developing sexual interests and concerns at an ever younger age and at an increasingly rapid pace. While it may be the case that, at least in part, children are maturing physically much sooner than did their parents and grandparents, I would suggest that before we conclude that this may the principal factor determining the rise of pre-teen sexual activity and pregnancy, it may be as relevant, if far more disturbing, to consider whether the ever-closer correspondence between childhood and adult attitudes and activities may be an equally important, or an even more significant, factor.

If so, then is it not likely that, just as children adopt more erotically-aware stances and lifestyles, they will also, as a consequence, engage in more adult-like sexual activities with each other? And if such activities are more commonly exhibited in the presence of adults who themselves have become more infantalized, then the very real – if undesirable – possibility of a mingling of child and adult participants in sexual games and behaviours becomes all the more likely. As such, might it not be, as Freud suggested so many years ago, that our most vociferous and violent reactions against those whom we label as 'perverts' and 'deviants' might be, in part, exacerbated by the unacceptable realization that precisely that which the 'pervert' and 'deviant' enacts expresses our own suppressed wishes and desires?

Again, let me be clear: even if this were so, it should not lead us to minimize or exculpate the actions, and their consequences, of those for whom suppression does not work. Rather, what is being asked is that we be more honest in considering the role that those of us who are 'sufficiently normal' may be playing in encouraging, however unthinkingly and unwillingly, abusive behaviour towards children. Provided with such an opportunity, child abusers might well convince themselves that their wants and needs (be they of companionship or sex, or both) are of an equivalent kind, and are shared by children whose ever more precariously maintained experience of 'childhood' will be brought to a sudden and infelicitous end by their oppressive acts.

If we are truly so concerned about securing the innocence

and dignity of childhood, it seems worthwhile to ask whether, at times, the adult's ever more insistent presence in children's lives might not be serving to prevent their very experience of being children.

7 Psychotherapy and the challenge of evil

It is all too easy to conjure up images of evil. Faced with such a task, my own mind provokes immediate and obvious thoughts of Pol Pot, Fred and Rosemary West, Pinochet, Stalin. Numerous competitors struggle for my attention, each raising up ever more explicit images of sickening brutality. I think of the violence enacted under the cause of political ideology, or religious faith, or racial and ethnic cleansing, or for purposes of economic expediency and the assertion of power. I think of clients who have been victimized by the rapist and the molester, whether a stranger or a once-trusted member of their family. I also think of those clients who were, themselves, the perpetrators of rape and molestation.

What unites such examples, and any number of others that can be brought to mind, is the notion of evil as a deliberate, wilful yet morally indefensible act of violence directed towards others. As an initial definition, it tends to be met with unguarded approval by media pundits, politicians and housing estate rabble-rousers intent upon expressing their revulsion and demanding swift retribution, easy answers. So many of us seem to 'know' what evil is, insofar as it is, above all else, something that *others* commit.

This chapter concerns itself with the question of evil as considered by psychotherapeutic theories. It challenges the psychotherapeutic tendency to avoid the moral and existential dimensions of evil via the transformative language of psychopathology which allows theorists and practitioners to rely (either implicitly or explicitly) upon metaphors of disease or immaturity – be they physical or psychic.

The views contained within this tendency, I believe, pose considerable quandaries not least because of the many problematic implications that arise from the adoption of these metaphors. Among these, as this chapter will argue, is the assumption that evil is best understood and seemingly explained from an individualistic intrapsychic perspective – which is to say: *evil lies within a being.*

Instead, I will attempt to present what will hopefully be seen to be a more adequate, if no less disturbing, interpersonally focused viewpoint. None the less, as I must state from the outset, I can offer no solution to the problem of evil. I suspect that, like so many other human attributes, while the careful scrutiny of our lived relationship with it can permit fresh insights and more humane possibilities, no amount of awareness and understanding, even if acted upon with diligence and care, will permit its eradication. As a way of beginning my exposition, I offer three personal 'statements' regarding my experience and understanding of evil.

First statement: Over the years during which I have lived in London, I have continued to bump into a street-person – let me call her Claudia – and have noted her progressive physical and mental degeneration. During one of our brief discussions, nearly a decade ago now, Claudia urged me to look at the passers-by from her perspective and stated, somewhat matter-of-factly, 'You know what's funny though? A lot of folks walk by and see me, but it's as if they don't. It's like I've turned invisible or something. Funny, that. It's odd to know that you exist but not to be recognized as existing.'

Her words have remained with me and, every once in a while, on those all-too-common occasions when I catch myself being just another person who walks by so many other 'Claudias', I remind myself not only of her but also of a passage from a book by Hannah Arendt entitled *Origins of Totalitari-*

anism.[1] Arendt makes the point that, during the Nazi regime, Jewish citizens, having been deprived of all their rights, their possessions, even the clothes off their backs, discovered that they had become non-beings. '*It seems*', Arendt wrote, '*that a man who is nothing but a man, has lost the very qualities which make it possible for other people to treat him as a fellow man.*'[2]

Second statement: In 1969, I found myself living for several weeks in London, Ontario in a house full of 'speed freaks'. I was playing detective, following the footsteps of my best friend who had disappeared, either to lick his wounds or to kill himself because of a failed romance. Of the nine human inhabitants of the household, the only one who disdained the proffered syringe of 'liquid crystal', besides myself, was the lunatic who refused to come out of his room unless it was full moon. The others felt sorry for me, sorry that, in spite of their benevolent offerings of free helpings to the drug, I persisted in rejecting their gift. As my room had the best daylight, it was the most desirable space in which to 'shoot up'. Day after day, throughout the entire time I lived there, all manner of people – residents and visitors, dealers and clients – trooped in, jacked up, felt the buzz.

Although I was not truly a part of them, the 'speed freaks' made me feel welcome, included me in their conversations, their banquets of stolen food and donated 'past their expiry date' helpings of bread and doughnuts picked up from a nearby bakery. They taught me how to caramelize sugar (the ultimate speed-freak delicacy), how to discern the relative purity of methedrine, what numerological meaning lay hidden in my name. However much I might have judged them, and the lives they led, to be screwed up or sad, on the whole, I judged them to be 'good people'.

Then, one night, while sitting with them, laughing and joking, by now hardly paying attention to their casual sharing of a needle, I noticed one of them grab the house cat and inject it with speed. In moments, the crazed creature was quite literally clawing its way up one of the walls, wailing in anything but ecstasy. Shocked by this senseless act of malice, I screamed at them, imploring them to explain why on earth they would carry out such evil on a helpless cat. They stared at me as if I was mad. How could I not see that the act was one of care and kindness? It was, they insisted, an attempt to elevate the cat's mental faculties, just as theirs had been elevated. It was, they screamed back, anything *but* evil.

Something of this stance infuses an important argument raised by George Steiner. Steiner has suggested that evil is best understood as the act of reaching out towards fulfilment. The deeds required to achieve this aim, considered abstractly, may be termed as evil by others, but to the being who enacts them they express the deluded, yet sincere, belief that they are necessary, even heroic, measures designed to either save or elevate self, or other, or indeed all of life from an intolerable or inadequate set of circumstances. Such a belief, Steiner proposes, succeeds in armouring the person against remorse, guilt, the acknowledgement that he or she has committed an evil act.[3] Thus, if, for instance, I see myself as a doctor ridding the world of disease, are my actions evil just because the 'disease' happens to be other human beings?

On further reflection, however, other, equally pertinent hypothetical possibilities begin to emerge. For, as the philosopher Berel Lang has proposed, what if it is also the case that the being who commits evil does so not out of some deluded sense of care or concern for self, others, or the world as a whole, but *'because he or she is fully aware that the intended act is, without doubt, evil?'*[4] In other words, can it not be that I – we – choose evil precisely because I – we – know that, regardless of its cost, it is evil alone that will satisfy?

Lang's ideas seem to me to be in keeping with my *third statement:* When I challenge myself to contemplate my own evil, my initial memories take me back to my childhood. I am ten years old and facing another child whom I currently loathe more than anyone else on the planet. A week ago, a day ago, perhaps, he was a close friend. He would come with me to the meadow behind my house, each of us carrying glass jars into which we would place newly captured grasshoppers. He made me laugh so hard because, one day, when opening one of these jars, now full of dozens of squirming grasshoppers, he inadvertently allowed one to attempt a sudden leap of freedom straight into his open mouth and, in reflexive, shocked surprise, swallowed the grasshopper live. Now, this same child, once my ally and friend, is my most hated enemy.

He is my enemy because he is demanding that I let him read a brand new comic book that is too precious for me to entrust to anyone, much less this obnoxious adversary. His demands become louder, more vicious. If I don't give him the comic book now, he threatens that he will tell my parents that I won't share my possessions and they will take it away from me. Suddenly, a grim solution to my dilemma presents itself to me. Almost gleefully, I take the comic book and rip it in half, startling both myself and my foe as much as had the grasshopper of days gone by. Perhaps more so. Then I begin to shout and wail so loudly that my parents and his parents rush into the room, see me clutching my now destroyed comic book, and arrive at the logical, if wildly incorrect, solution. Before my eyes, my still-startled enemy receives the spanking of his life. That I feel joy at having vanquished my antagonist so effectively is without doubt, but it is a joy brought forth by evil. It has cost me dearly, dearer than the price and pleasure of a favoured comic book that even my joy is not able to make whole once again. And, of course, it is not simply the shredded comic book that has been damaged beyond repair.

Taken together, it seems to me that these three statements capture the principal boundaries of evil: evil acts committed through indifference, through arrogance and error of judgement and through purposeful intent. How might we begin to make sense of a set of actions so wide-ranging and yet so easily available that even a child can grasp their possibilities?

It is rare to find in psychotherapeutic literature any extended analysis or discussion that directly concerns itself with the notion of *evil*. Psychotherapists appear to be somewhat reluctant to employ the word as part of their vocabulary. They prefer, instead, to utilize the language of psychopathology, sociopathy, personality disorders. Such language serves to reduce or remove their discourse from the moral dimensions – and quandaries – of *being human*.

To be fair, various psychotherapists have faced the dilemma of evil head-on, arguing that the questions it raises are of as much import to psychology as they are to theological debate. Both Sigmund Freud and Carl Jung considered the question as did, more recently, Carl Rogers and Rollo May.[5] From such debates have emerged two broad, if mutually antagonistic viewpoints. The first asserts that evil acts are expressions of a basic, in-built tendency (or drive, or instinct) that can be surmised to exist within all human beings. The second perspective, on the other hand, insists that expressions of evil are alien to human nature and, instead, must be understood solely in terms of behavioural reactions to a wide range of intolerable internal conflicts arising in reaction to any number of inadequate or warped social demands and restrictions placed upon the individual.[6] While both positions point us towards important and valid arenas for further consideration such that neither should be dismissed out of hand, none the less it is of significance to note that while their disagreements are apparent, a more subtle point of accord between them also emerges: that it is this subjective conflict or weakness within the psyche of an individual that is, ultimately, responsible for the presence of evil.

The history of psychotherapy illuminates a crucial cultural shift in understanding and dealing with disruptive and disturbing behaviour. While the genesis of this had once been assumed to be due to *extrapsychic agencies* (namely, external forces, be they natural or supernatural) that have possessed the sufferer's mind or soul, an alternative view suggesting that the basis was to be understood and treated from the standpoint of *intrapsychic agencies* (the disturbances of brain and mind) eventually supplanted the earlier hypothesis.[7] This reassessment has its implications for our explanations of evil. For evil, too, if understood as a disturbance of thought, behaviour and/or affect, must, like other disturbances, also be seen to be a product of intrapsychic conflict for which each being is responsible. Almost the entire body of therapeutic literature, whether considered from the viewpoint of psychoanalysis, analytical psychology, or even forensic psychiatry, assumes this intrapsychic hypothesis.

For example, intrapsychic assumptions continue to dominate the many contrasting theories put forward by psychologists and psychotherapists who have attempted to explain the genesis of Adolf Hitler's psychopathology.[8] What is most fascinating to me about these psychotherapeutic attempts to explain Hitler's evil is that not one of the conjectures proffered is able to make a strong enough argument as to why such an extreme – perhaps even ultimate – expression of evil could, and did, come about. Insufficient case after case has been made to explain Hitler's psychopathology as a result of – take your pick – paternal violence; maternal over-protectiveness; childhood trauma due to an over-eager goat's successful attempt at biting off one of young Hitler's testicles; sexual inadequacy resulting from an organically derived testicular defect; a narcissistic borderline personality disorder; an overabundant Thanatos drive; an unspecified, but unusual, libidinal disturbance. Alternatively, as if it were a sufficient explanation in itself, the hypothesis of Hitler being the world's first serial killer has also been put forward.[9]

The critical problem with each and every one of these deductions lies in its inability to demonstrate any *unique*

factors that could have brought about such a uniquely disturbed individual. Yet such explanations require unique factors in order for them to be of any worth. For, if no unique
factors exist, it becomes at least questionable to continue to
assert Hitler's unique qualities of evil. And if Hitlerian evil is
not unique? Well, then a dreadful possibility begins to emerge
since, in order for us to be able to explain him in ways which
validate our current views, he must be made more like us, just
as we must be made more like him. In answer to the question
'Was Hitler evil?', the historian Alan Bullock recently replied,
'*If he isn't evil, who is?*'[10] Exactly.

While it may be disquieting for us to consider this last
consequence, important, if much criticized (on grounds of the
ethical issues raised for some) findings by social scientists
point us in all too similar directions. Stanley Milgram's studies
on ordinary individuals' willingness to obey even dubious
forms of authority reveal their decision to comply with socially
organized and personally induced forms of torture upon other
human beings.[11] In like fashion, Paul Zimbardo and his asso-
ciates' filmed experiments dealing with university students'
increasingly violent 'role-playing' as prison guards controlling
the behaviour of their convicts (fellow students) show all too
clearly how easily even the most educated among us are
prepared to devise and inflict torture upon others.[12] In
addition, recent historical research such as Daniel Goldhagen's
Hitler's Willing Executioners reveals the extent to which so
many ordinary German citizens, regardless of social class or
profession, were knowingly involved in the atrocities committed by the Nazis.[13] These examples, and many more like them,
make plain that we are not required to dredge up a Caligula or
a Milosevic in order to contemplate the disturbing possibilities
of evil. Rather, as these studies make all too clear, evil can be
enacted with surprising ease by even the most normal and
sanest of men and women.

However, it is not merely research that might sway us

towards the consideration of such unedifying possibilities. Our society is so fascinated by evil that every form of butchery and brutality is trumpeted and picked over by our newspapers and television broadcasts. Serial killers and sociopaths, poorly reared children and confused teenagers, fine, upstanding citizens, 'good people' who turned out not to be – are all grist to the mill of popular fiction, cinema, our daily lives. Could it be that such accounts of evil so effortlessly capture and retain our interest not because the perpetrators appear to be so alien, so different from us, but rather because they provoke a sense of queasy kinship?

The following passage written recently by Hilary Mantel in a review of Gitta Sereny's biography of the child-killer (in both senses of the term) Mary Bell provides a possible answer:

> **But part of us wants more information . . . to feed our fascination and fear. What is it that we fear? Not the loss to the victim, but the loss of innocence in ourselves; not her loss of control, but the fragility of it in ourselves. We can, as Gitta Sereny suggests 'use' Mary, less to confirm our faith in society than to confirm the daily wonder that we believe in society at all. We can, with effort, see Mary not as an alien, but Mary as kin, as a stained and transgressive being like us: with *the malady of being human, and with no hope of a cure* [emphasis added].[14]**

None the less, the idea of a despot like Hitler *being just like all the rest of us* also fails to succeed in ringing quite true. Considering Hitler's specific acts of evil, and without either intended disrespect or desire to bracket the moral repugnance that they must surely provoke, it remains evident that Hitler's evil reveals a terrifying originality and inventiveness, a twisted version of genius that patently contradicts Hannah Arendt's now famous argument regarding 'the banality of evil'.[15] Prior to Hitler's actualization of his evil intentions, no one could have seriously predicted that such acts *would* take place. And, equally, it must be said, that while it is the case that, since Hitler, various odious imitators have emerged, none has equalled, much less surpassed, his dreadful work. Yet, if we follow this path, we are presented with a persistent explanatory gap. As much as we ask 'why?', no sufficiently explanatory 'why' emerges.

This state of affairs provokes a resonance of sorts with Primo Levi's account of his confrontation with an SS Guard while he was imprisoned in Auschwitz. Pointing to the degradation and inhumanity that is all too apparent, Levi asks his tormentor 'Why?' The Guard's response is as significant as it is disgusting: '*There is no* why *here*'.[16]

This statement reminds me of a client, Victor, a film director, who, all too aware of my own fascination with this medium, one day, asks me: 'What is the best example of an existential film?' The question both intrigues and throws me. It is not one I have asked myself before. Numerous, somewhat obvious, possibilities vie for my attention, distance me from my encounter with Victor. Realizing this, I play the parody of a psychotherapist. 'What is it to you?' I reply. For his own reason or benefit, Victor deigns to provide me with his answer. 'It's obvious,' he says. 'It's Peckinpah's film, *The Wild Bunch*. Nothing else comes close.' I think of the film: death in slow motion, Hollywood's discovery that men bleed – and bleed profusely – when they are shot. 'You mean,' I venture, 'its emphasis on death?'

'Don't take me for an idiot!' Victor snaps. 'No, I don't mean "its emphasis on death",' he parrots back. Instead, he explains what he means is that the circular structure of the film begins and ends with a major act of violence resulting in scores of corpses, but, on reflection, an all too significant difference becomes apparent. When the central characters initiate the violence at the start of the film, they do so because they have lost all meaning, all purpose, all sense of belonging, all sense of care, in their lives. When that slaughter begins, each thinks only of himself; each death of a member of *The Bunch* just means a larger share of the bounty, a greater chance of dodging the bullet, for the rest. By the end of the film, however, something has happened. A meaning of sorts has emerged: One of *The Bunch* has been captured and tortured by a Mexican General and his misfit army. No money, no guns that *The Bunch* can offer is enough for them to buy him back. A phrase muttered earlier in the film now returns to haunt them: '*It's not about "giving your word"; it's who you give it to, that counts*'.[17]

Facing up to a law that is of their own making, *The Bunch* at last acknowledge their responsibilities as men. 'Let's do it,' one says. 'Why not?' comes the reply. Together, united, they confront their enemy, ask for their comrade. In response, the General slits their friend's throat, instantly killing him. *The Bunch*'s reaction is not impulsive; for a long, nearly endless moment, all action, even the film itself, appears to freeze into stasis. Then the choice is made. Guns blaze. More blood. More death. The remnants of *The Bunch* kill and are killed. And if *The Bunch* revel in the decision they have made and its consequences, none the less, at the moment of their death, the pointlessness and inevitability of their actions provokes their frightened whimpers. Just in case the audience has missed this final point, Peckinpah inserts a coda to the story. Vultures – both animal and human – descend to pick at the carcasses. If *The Bunch*'s final act has any meaning, it is for them alone. The world goes on unchanged. More death – be it senseless or meaningful, peaceful or brutal, evil or heroic – will follow.

The world of *The Wild Bunch* is unrelentingly evil. Not one character in the entire film, not even the children portrayed, is spared. How skewed is this reel reflection of the real world? Thinking about *The Wild Bunch*, I consider the very real butchery and brutality – the evil – that is so easily found in our newspaper headlines and daily lives. I find myself imagining the high school kids from Columbine, Colorado, dressed in their leather coats, looking almost like something out of a

Hollywood western. Another 'Wild Bunch', perhaps, not just in style and location, but something far more significant.

Did their empty lives find sudden and singular meaning in their acts of evil? Is the 'why?' of evil all too similar to the 'Big Why?' we ask ourselves? Could this be why accounts of evil so easily capture and retain our interest – not because they raise questions but, perhaps, because they provide some sort of answer? Or, just as possibly, no answer at all? There is no '*why*' here. It is because it is 'the malady of being human, and with no hope of a cure'. If we follow this path, are we not once more re-entering the territory of psychotherapy?

Psychotherapists have tended to adopt a view towards the issue of evil that can be considered as some sort of moral cretinism, in that it is not so much an indication of an alien inhuman otherness as a less highly evolved form of human-ness.[18] What psychotherapists fail to realize is that in taking such views they mimic the separatist attitudes of those very same 'evil' beings who permit themselves to label their victims as being *less than fully human*. However inadvertently, the language of psychotherapy promotes a more subtle version of this same separatist distinctiveness in order to make sense of the acts of brutality and violence of those beings whom they analyse. For, just as the former, by one means or another, succeed in reducing their victims to some sort of subhuman level, so do psychotherapists slyly achieve much the same through their hypotheses and specialist language that rely upon simplistic views regarding genes for criminality or vio-lence, or which rest upon more complex notions of arrested psychic development.

Psychotherapists seek out intrapsychic causes to explain evil. And if such causes are not easily forthcoming? Well, then they rely upon their talent as psychotherapists: they are, after all, artists of invention. Rogue genes, inadequate environ-ments, intolerable levels of sexual and/or physical abuse, unconscious conflicts – whatever sounds feasible enough to convince them, and, in turn, to convince their clients, their trainees, the public media that an adequate explanation has been provided.

However, a worrisome question must be faced: in adhering to the theories that psychotherapists typically advocate, do they actually have anything of worth to offer? Or is it, sadly, the case that what is stated merely serves to maintain vapid explanations which, on reflection, explain little at all, and instead encourage and preserve an inadequate and ruinous faith in illusory ideas, idle chatter, promoted by false – and self-interested – prophets?

The existential philosopher Martin Heidegger, whose own self-serving choice to espouse the Nazi Party and its policies aptly also provokes this dissonant experience for so many of us, pointed out that the original meaning of truth was derived from the Greek notion of *aletheia* – the unconcealedness, or unveiledness, the transparent presence, of beings. It was only in later times that truth came to be associated with the correctness of an assertion. With such a significant shift in meaning, according to Heidegger, truth became a primary instrument towards the objectification and technologization of being.[19]

An unconcealed being is revealed as complex, contradictory, open to myriad paradoxical possibilities. Such a 'truth' runs counter to the 'truth' of our current culture whose preferred dichotomies are simple, straightforward: correct or incorrect, right or wrong, good or evil. Yet which of these notions of truth more adequately expresses our interrelational experience of self and others?

Of course, truth understood as a correct assertion allows us to act – or not act – from a standpoint of security, of assertive certainty. We can know what is right and proper, or wrong and improper, or, at least, we maintain the pretence that permits us to claim that we know.

It may be the case that various Eastern philosophies have arrived at a view of truth that is more in keeping with the notion of aletheia. Recently, for instance, it was reported that The Dalai Lama could not understand why contemporary Western physicists remain so disturbed by the experimental data which force them to the conclusion that quantum potentialities express themselves equally well as both waves and particles, until he realized that Western minds appear not to have yet established a logic that can allow contradictory opposites to be true at the same time.[20] Considered more generally, this specific dilemma, it appears to me, presents itself in myriad ways in the language and beliefs of contemporary psychotherapy such that its truths are revealed to be, at best, limited. The exploration of big issues – such as the question of evil – might well provoke the realization that these self-same theories, as well as being limited, may also be redundant. Perhaps this is one reason why psychotherapists tend to avoid tackling these matters.

What persists in eluding us, it seems, is the capacity to maintain a view that is both contradictory and yet can access and hold such contradictions simultaneously in time – without recourse to hypotheses regarding an avowed separate unconscious system. I would suggest that this view shares some pertinent similarities with the ideas regarding the self-structure, and its sedimentations and dissociations, discussed in previous chapters. Certainly, what points of commonality exist highlight the possibility of maintaining divided stances at a conscious level of interrelationally lived experiences. Might it not be the case that our stances towards evil might be more adequately considered from this perspective?

Recall the point made by Friedrich Nietzsche that I discussed briefly in Chapter 1: so long as you are *seen* to believe in a supposed truth with sufficient conviction and passion, others will come to believe in it as well. In turn, even if you yourself once harboured doubts about your beliefs, now the certainty of others in your truths, in you, yourself, will eradicate all doubt.[21]

This temporality and circularity of truth-creation takes us away from the more simplistic linear equations favoured by psychotherapists, just as it also challenges our biased tendency to consider the solution of dilemmas in terms of inner or outer forces, conflicts or aberrations. Perhaps most significantly, Nietzsche's insight places the maintenance of and adherence to truths within an interrelational realm, something that is neither entirely owned by self or other alone, but by both in their relationship to and with one another.

If we were to take Nietzsche's analysis and replace the word 'truth' in the above statement with the word 'evil', might we not be equally, if unwillingly, confronted with the realization of evil's interrelational qualities? Furthermore, would not this shift expose the inadequacies of psychotherapeutic responses, such as they are, which typically continue to rely upon and emphasize elusive intrapsychic factors and forces that express themselves in contradictory (if hidden) fashion to our conscious stances and explanations as the necessary foundations to the understanding of the problem of evil?

While dilemmas such as the question of evil may well have no absolute solution, challenging ourselves with regard to how we respond to them remains not merely worthwhile, but pivotal. And in this enterprise, surely, psychotherapists might have something to offer – *if* they were prepared to acknowledge that psychotherapeutic expertise lies within the realm of an aletheic truth that manifests itself through interpersonal encounters.

When it comes to the possibility of evil, perhaps, in their uncertainty, our questions will none the less serve both to implicate and expose the questioner – and the focus of our questioning – to more honest scrutiny. Perhaps continuing to ask the questions in ways that permit novel 'mirrors' to reflect and reveal uncomfortable truths will prove to be the best we can do.

8 Creation and being: a challenge to psychoanalytic theories of artistic creativity

Why do human beings attempt to create *works of art*? What is the nature of the value placed upon the works by their audience? What do the individual artistic creator and audience member experience through works of art that is so compelling and meaningful to them? What kind of person does it take to become an artistic creator of merit and genius? And how is it that works of art are not universally recognized as being such or, similarly, may undergo reassessment or be discovered for the first time by later generations or by other cultures alien to that in which the creative artist lived and produced the work in question?

All manner of responses to any, or all of these questions can readily spring to mind. For instance, with regard to the 'why' of creativity, one could invoke rationales focused upon such factors as the accumulation of wealth, fame, self-esteem, the increasing likelihood of easily available and inventive forms of sexual gratification. And, it is true, it would not be difficult to conjure up numerous illustrations in favour of this argument.

In similar fashion, one could argue that these same possibilities might explain the 'why' of the audience member. After all, various examples also exist of the critic, the manager, the agent, the impresario, the benefactor (all of whom, after all, can be designated as members of the audience) who achieves power, wealth and fame (and the sexual desirability associated with such features) to match – if not surpass – that of the creative artist. On further reflection, even the more 'ordinary' members of the audience might benefit in similar ways simply by associating and identifying themselves with the artist and the work. Further, if such associations and identifications are made by sufficiently large numbers of individuals, as a group (of 'followers' and 'fans'), they might set about generating and attaining something that approaches the same rewards on offer to the artist. Such an explanation is, of course, at best only partially correct. Just as we can generate numerous examples that 'fit' this conclusion, all manner of contradictory alternatives (not least those that invoke images of artists who have remained unknown and unappreciated within their lifetime) will also arise.

These inconclusive and contradictory possibilities remain a constant for whatever explanations we put forward regarding artistic creativity. For every artist who declares that the answer lies in the fact that he or she is *compelled* to create, we find an alternative perspective which declares that 'It is just something I'm able to do'.

As a species, we devote a great deal of time and effort in seeking out works of art that will please, excite, disturb, elevate or permit regression to 'more primitive' states of mind. And while it is commonly argued that artistic creativity provides no direct, nor easily discernible, survival value to us, either as individuals or as a species as a whole, our fascination with all (and continuously evolving) forms of artistic creativity reveals its power – regardless of cultural diversity or historical era.

For example, in today's society, although only a small number of individuals are labelled and lauded as *artists*, the majority of the population embraces and participates in numerous expressions of what might be termed as a form of *popular art* that is accessible to all: the adorning of bodies with unique combinations of clothing and jewellery, the current fascination with the dyeing and piercing of skin, the various arrangements and rearrangements of one's private environment, whether it be internal (i.e. decorating) or external (i.e. gardening) – all such expressions, and a great deal more, can be seen as aspects of artistic creativity.[1]

Unfortunately, our attempts to answer why we lavish so much care and attention upon artistic activities remains a focus of disturbance, debate and division.

Over the past century, Western ideas surrounding the meaning and purpose of artistic creativity have become increasingly influenced, if not dominated, by psychoanalytic hypotheses. Indeed, every major psychoanalyst, beginning with Sigmund Freud himself, has made attempts to explain the psychological basis to this distinctly human tendency and, just as various alterations and competing views have evolved within psychoanalytic theory itself, so too have these been utilized as springboards to the diversity of theories this diffuse model has put forward concerning the 'why' of creation. To be sure, many of the opinions put forward are fascinating and engaging to artists as well as to their audiences and, if only for this reason, require genuine appraisal. However, one overwhelming tendency, implicitly advocated by all psychoanalytic perspectives, has taken root and flourished over time and it is this particular trend that has increasingly become of concern to numerous critics of psychoanalysis, myself included.

Briefly summarized, this recurring pattern places its emphasis upon the personality and history of an individual artist as the key factor towards the understanding of artistic creativity. The success of this inclination is such that, for many experts and interested laypersons, it has become the principal, if not sole, strategy to be employed in formulating our hypotheses. We assume, for instance, that if we know more about the life circumstances of someone like Mozart or Rodin or Van Gogh or Fellini, we will be in a better position to appreciate the products of that person's creativity and, as well, we will be better placed to understand the 'why' of artistic creativity both in its particular and general instances. Indeed, we have learned to *impose* our knowledge of the person (even when that knowledge is second-, third- or fourth-hand) upon that which the person has chosen to offer the world.

This way of thinking about artistic creativity (or any form of creativity in general) has come to dominate twentieth-present day cultural enquiry and criticism. While nineteenth-century Romanticism inspired 'the cult of the artist', it was not until the twentieth century that such enquiries into the minutiae of all aspects of the personal and private lives of artists would become so prevalent that most contemporary critics (not to mention audiences) can imagine little that is more pertinent or natural to their investigations. However, in acknowledging these concerns, let me return to the critical conundrum: What motivates all expressions of artistic creativity?

This question was not first asked by Freud and his followers but is a far more ancient quandary. Plato, for instance, argued that the artist creates through *divine intervention* during which time the artist's rational faculties yield to irrational frenzies.[2] In contrast, Aristotle formulated the notion of the artist as a *skilled craftsman* who practised a controlled, intentional activity designed to express workmanship.[3] While these contradictory perspectives have appeared and reappeared in differing guises over the centuries, and while it is evident that both views dominate our current thinking, it is the former view which, in replacing 'divine intervention' with 'unconscious turbulence', principally engages psychoanalytic thought.

Freud's 'answer' to the questions raised by artistic creativity was to turn his – and our – attention to the artist's *personality*. In doing so, he was able to argue the view that the creative person has exceptionally powerful and frustrated instinctual drives and an extraordinary capacity to sublimate or rechannel them into artistic activity and product. The aim and objective of creation therefore serves as the means by which the artist seeks to cope with unconscious Oedipal wishes that can neither be directly enacted nor consciously accepted. As with the symptoms of the neurotic, artistic expression serves as a defence mechanism which channels and distorts unconscious wishes so that the energy associated with them is sublimated into socially sanctioned activity and product. Similarly, just as the make-up and specificity of the neurotic symptom also acts out its hidden source of disturbance, so, too, according to Freud, does the form and content of the artistic product reveal – at least to those psychoanalytic experts who are trained to look in particular ways – the specific disturbance with which the artist has grappled.[4] Not surprisingly, and, if one accepts his theory, of particular pertinence to Freud's own set of psychic disturbances, Oedipal conflicts and the theme of parricide are prominent recurring motifs in Freud's own writings on artistic creativity.[5]

In addition, Freud argues that the basis for the social sanctioning of artistic endeavours lies in the audience's experiences of its own unconscious gratification when exposed to works of art. First, writes Freud, the audience experiences such gratification in the form of a fore-pleasure in its pleasurable (or, more specifically, erotic) responses to the formal properties of the work. Second, and far more significantly, the audience experiences pleasure in the act of unconsciously deciphering the unconscious content and themes that the work contains and which the audience itself shares at an unconscious level.[6]

Many problems have emerged with regard to Freud's theory. Not least among them is why so few people turn towards such an obviously satisfactory means of sublimation. Again, Freud's reply – that artists suffer from particularly powerful instinctual wishes – reveals a flawed – and, as usual, *circular* – argument: both the notion of 'the artist' and the notion of what constitutes 'particularly powerful instinctual wishes' rely upon and require one another for their own and the other's definition in order for the theory to stand. In its circularity, Freud's account reveals itself as a theory that cannot be falsified.[7]

Further, Freud's approach dismisses the whole question of aesthetics in that he is unable to tell us why any particular work is distinguished as an example of art rather than a sort of uninteresting *personal masturbation*. Indeed, Freud's theory cannot truly distinguish one from the other since both are equally reliant upon the same unconscious conflicts. Similarly, if Freud is interested in the content of the work as a means of exposing such conflicts in terms of the artist's repressed infantile concerns, he can say nothing about the artist's chosen medium of expression. As Anthony Storr puts it: '*the weakness of psychoanalytic interpretations of works of art is twofold. Psychoanalysis neither distinguished between bad art and good; nor, more importantly, between a work of art and a neurotic symptom.*'[8]

There exists a further implicit problem for Freud's theory: if he is correct, then it should be the case that the artist who undergoes successful psychoanalysis will experience a decrease in the desire to create. What evidence exists on this matter suggests that either no artist has yet to experience a successful psychoanalysis, or the accumulated data at best fail to confirm, and at worst entirely contradict, this hypothesis.[9]

Nevertheless, while Freud's theory proves to be unsatisfactory as a whole, one aspect of it has been particularly developed and extended. As expressed in Freud's paper, '*The relation of the poet to day-dreaming*', this is the notion that artistic activity bears striking similarities to childhood play activity in that, through each, the artist/child creates a world of fantasy which he or she treats with the utmost seriousness and import, invests a great deal of emotion, and which allows a separation from everyday reality.[10] Such a view still does not begin to explain how we might distinguish between 'good' and 'bad' art, but it does offer us the potentially useful proposition that playing and creativity at the very least share important functional similarities. I will return to this issue later in the chapter.

Psychoanalytic authors since Freud have maintained their focus upon those themes that Freud insisted were central to the understanding of the artist and his or her relation to the work. While disagreeing with him in specific – and pertinent – arenas, it remains the case that their general aim has remained largely unchanged.

Thus, for instance, some psychoanalysts have focused upon the different stages and lengths of the creative *incubation period*[11] while others have explored the *compulsive* elements of artistic creativity.[12] To be fair, such perspectives are commonly shared by artists themselves who, for instance, when asked why they create, are likely to respond: '*I have to.*'[13] Perhaps of the greatest significance, however, to the development of psychoanalytic concerns regarding artistic creativity since Freud's own speculations have been the various expositions regarding the relation of artistic activity to *anxiety*, whether it be in terms of the attempted alleviation of perceived threats from within (that is to say, originating from one's conscience) or from without (the perceived dictates and demands of others).

Anthony Storr's significant contribution to this strand in thought both relies upon, and extrapolates from, key ideas found in the work of two major psychoanalysts: W. R. D. Fairbairn and Melanie Klein. Storr argues that both authors highlighted the existence of two fundamental characterological temperaments that serve as defences against the primal anxiety of the 'split' between self and others. These two temperaments are labelled as: *the manic-depressive* and *the schizoid*. While the former temperament's principal defences recognize the existence of this 'split' and seek to re-create a 'pre-split' reality by eliminating all disharmony and disjunction between self and others, the latter temperament defends against these anxieties via its denial of this split and its concomitant insistence upon the maintenance of a 'pre-split' fantasy.[14]

As Storr suggests, when placed within the specific question of artistic creativity, this characterological conjecture provides us with a set of intriguing hypotheses, of which the following may be the most pertinent.

1 That creative individuals can be demonstrably distinguished as being of predominant manic-depressive or schizoid temperaments.
2 That certain types of creative thought, activity and product are only possible for one type of temperament and not for the other.
3 That the importance given by the artist to his or her work becomes understandable in that it is a need – much like that of the addict – that must be enacted in order to offset states of foundational intrapsychic anxiety.

If we consider the manic-depressive individual's advantages in being an artist, the following possibilities become apparent.

Just as *the manic-depressive temperament* in general yearns for the world's recognition and approval so that the acknowledged 'split' between self and world is experienced as secure and unthreatening, for the manic-depressive artist the high regard and value placed by the world upon what it deems to be successful or worthy artistic creativity makes the possibility of his or her experience of a steady level of maintenance of self-esteem through artistic activity a highly desirable option. The fundamental attitude of aggression directed towards the world or towards the self characteristic of the manic-depressive temperament can be safely expressed by the manic-depressive artist – with the added bonus that the world will, however unwittingly, also grant its appreciation and request even more of his or her unsparing criticism. In like fashion, the manic-depressive artist's insatiable demands for world-directed self-esteem can be displaced into the artistic activity and its product such that these not only become the principal undertaking in his or her daily routine but also take precedence over all other enterprises – including the maintenance of the artist's own health and well-being. Further, the primary aspects of the manic-depressive temperament (such as frequent bursts of overactivity followed by listlessness and indolence, moments of overly empathetic concern for others that are succeeded by sudden and over-reactive irritability with the perceived stupidities and human failings of others, states of high elation and the certainty of one's ability to surmount all obstacles segueing towards depths of despair and extreme expressions of self-directed loathing) can all be accommodated within the 'social role' of being an artist. Finally, the manic-depressive's primary anxieties concerning the life-threatening demands of the world can be temporarily eliminated by the artist's thematic focus upon, and representations of, both the myriad menaces of an unbalanced social or natural world order and the desirable possibilities of a harmonious external reality whose symmetry reflects an ultimate equilibrium between self and others.

On the other hand, the *schizoid temperament*'s need for isolation and avoidance of the acknowledgement of a separate world in order more easily to permit at least the partial retention of his or her fantasy of omnipotence can be maintained by the schizoid artist through the recognition that the creative act is principally solitary and cocooned from the influences and demands of everyday social activities and relations. In addition, the far greater import given to inner reality rather than to the external world that is the primary stance of those dominated by a schizoid temperament can be expressed by the schizoid artist's imaginative invention of a meaningful world of which he or she is its guiding creator, whose sets of values serve as direct reflections of those of the artist, and whose 'reality', in turn, can be maintained with relatively little hindrance and threat from the intrusions and challenges of others. Further, the schizoid's predominant anxieties regarding the arbitrary unpredictability and meaninglessness of the world, whose acknowledgement is in itself psychically intolerable, can be allayed by the artist's creation of a separate and unique world that, as well as being more adequately meaningful, can be, in part, controlled and made sufficiently secure and whose presence encourages entry rather than avoidance and denial. Finally, as with the manic-depressive temperament but in its opposite direction, the schizoid's sense of security and abeyance from anxiety is brought about by a focus upon the internal and subjective that serve to retain the fantasy of an existence prior to its 'split' into a world of self and others. This need can be, in part, expressed and preserved through the specific thematic concerns of the schizoid artist's work which, typically, will be on the exposition of the abstract and mental dimensions of lived experience and which will be produced as and when the maintenance of this pre-split world is threatened by the anxiety-provoking intrusions of a 'post-split' reality.

As interesting and potentially revelatory as these views might be, it remains the case that in their adoption of an *intrapsychic* perspective focused upon the personality of the artist, they transform and, in part, reduce the act of artistic creation to a defensive strategy that, by implication, requires attention and treatment.

This critical turn, whether viewed with alarm or elation, reveals all too plainly that, via the psychoanalytic impetus, our interest has shifted principally to the exploration of the *intrapsychic conflicts of the creator* rather than remaining focused upon the created product itself. Indeed, the current predominance of this view has led us to suppose that the best, if not sole means through which we can appreciate a work of art is via our understanding of the life of its creator.

An obvious, if significant, indication of the general acceptance of this perspective can be ascertained through our ever-
increasing interest in the *biographies* of creative people. At the
same time, however, the inherent limitations of this creator-
focused stance towards artistic creativity also become apparent. For one thing, it seems to me to be both worrisome and
antagonistic to the dialogical possibilities of an interchange
between an artistic product and its audience to find that we
have reached a point where more and more people know
something of the lives and personalities of, say, Sylvia Plath,
Pablo Picasso, Jacqueline du Pré, Derek Jarman or Jack Kerouac
than will have read, listened to, contemplated or engaged with
their works. Related to this point, might it not be the case that
the audience's unceasing – and quite literal – pursuit of
reclusive artists and authors such as J. D. Salinger and Thomas
Pynchon just so that they can find out 'who they are and what
they look like' serves as an extension of the assumed importance we have placed upon the artist's personality as *the* critical
factor in our understanding and appreciation of his or her
work?

Worse still, the audience's acceptance of such personality-
focused analyses and assumptions has passed to the artists
themselves who, in turn, have been so drawn to these ideas
and influences that artistic activity has increasingly become
less focused upon product and, instead, has concerned itself
with narcissist self-promotion, and the egotistic assertion that
'It is who I am that matters. And who I am is so much more
interesting, and so much more important than who you are!'
Indeed, thanks to the 'post-structural' influences of theorists
such as Paul de Man and Jacques Derrida, we have taken such
glorification of the individual artists so far that even the lives
of the artistic creators have assumed secondary significance to
the deconstructive analysis of the biographer's set of cultural
values and biases. Nowadays, some would have it, it is no

longer the work or the artist but, rather, *the biographer* and *the critic* who should be (perhaps already are) the primary focus of our interest and attention.[15] How much has psychoanalysis cajoled us into taking this particular path? Are such Freudian-derived conceits a dead-end? Are there any valid alternatives?

Let me begin to answer such questions with an existential-phenomenological assertion: artistic creativity is not solely explicable in terms of psychopathology that it can be sufficiently understood as a displaced substitute for the satisfaction of a more fundamental drive or as an expression of intrapsychic conflict. Instead, as has been argued by Martin Heidegger, human creativity is to be understood as *an act of revelation or unconcealedness* regarding the truth of our existence; it is the means of 'unveiling' that which is present but is also ordinarily hidden from everyday awareness. Expressions of art are able to bring us *the truth of being*.[16]

However, for Heidegger, 'truth' is not 'the correctness of an assertion'. Rather, as was discussed in Chapter 7, Heidegger points us to the original meaning of truth: the Greek term *aletheia*, meaning the unconcealedness, the transparent presence of beings. As such, our engagement with a work of art permits us to take the time, and provides us with a language, to examine and respond to what is there in its unconcealedness. Think, for instance, of the many times you may have said to yourself or to others: 'This book/song/painting/poem manages to express what I knew or felt but for which I could not previously find the language.'

Heidegger's argument immediately moves us away from an emphasis upon the creator, or how the creative work was conceived and accomplished – since these queries serve to bring us back to a more everyday realm of concealedness – and instead focuses upon the revelatory possibilities inherent in the work itself. Similarly, there is, in Heidegger's approach, an implicit concern with the *universalities* of artistic creativity rather than a focus upon the idiosyncratic qualities of the creator.[17]

Heidegger links his argument regarding artistic creativity to a wider thesis regarding *language*. He objects to the more conventional notion that language merely serves to represent nature and suggests that to limit language in this way serves to reduce language to a '*composite of signs and symbols, rules of grammar, and forms of syntax*'.[18] Instead, Heidegger supposes that, if we are ever to get to grips with language we have to undergo an experience with language through the act of employing it.

> **To undergo an experience with something – be it a thing, a person, a God – means that this something befalls us, strikes us, comes over us, overwhelms and transforms us. When we talk of undergoing an experience, we mean that the experience is not of our making; to undergo here means rather to endure it, suffer it, receive it as it strikes us and submit to it.[19]**

There exist meanings and possibilities in Heidegger's exploration of artistic creativity that cannot be found in any parallel psychoanalytic account. He frees us from considering artistic endeavours as being merely backward-focused symbolic returns to, and repetitions of, hidden conflicts, and instead emphasizes the forward-looking, transformative potential presented to us. We suffer our artistic endeavours, just as we suffer language, in order that both we and the world may be revealed and transformed. And, while, admittedly, Heidegger speaks to us in somewhat lofty tones, is it not the case that we can discern in his words a restatement of that which not only so many artists themselves use when we invite them to tell us about their experience of being creative but also that, in similar fashion, we, as the audience engaged in dialogue with the work, feel in its presence?

Following Heidegger, we can argue that an existential-phenomenological examination of artistic creativity highlights its *illuminative quality* as being far more important than the regressive aspects emphasized by psychoanalysis. In doing so, it suggests a view of artistic creativity as an intense commitment – not a reconstruction of what is experienced but a new awareness that conveys to all who will attune themselves to it a novel truth concerning being.

This is not to say that there is nothing whatever of worth to be gained from considering issues of artistic creativity from a psychoanalytic perspective. On the contrary, various hypotheses, not least those dealing with artists' anxieties with regard to their self/world relations (as summarized above) are undoubtedly significant whether considered from an intrapsychic perspective or from the interpersonal standpoint preferred by existential authors. None the less, the answers they provide fail to address what may well be issues of far greater magnitude and relevance – what Heidegger expressed as '*the becoming and happening of truth*'.[20]

This focus upon a forward – even transformative – movement arising from a state of commitment returns us to a re-examination of the relationship between artistic creativity and play. Here again, although Freud principally focuses upon both play and artistic activity as forms of 'escape', more recent developmental psychologists (including some psychoanalytic authors) have emphasized different aspects of play activity such as the attempt to create an integral whole out of one's experience, and the effort to know and understand more deeply, penetrating beyond the surface of an activity towards a richer awareness.[21] Such views suggest significant resonances with artistic creativity: both activities appear to be apart from or not directly associated with the immediate satisfaction of biological needs; both are concerned with rule and ritual; both serve as means to discover and test out novel possibilities; both stimulate alertness. Following Heidegger, artistic creativity encourages free play of our being possibilities.[22]

While acts of creation, like play, may well permit the means to escape from disturbing realities and their concomitant anxieties, they nevertheless retain an inherent *'forwardness towards unconcealment'* that permits the exploration of novel interrelational possibilities. Rollo May has addressed the matter by taking the view that artistic creativity is best understood as an encounter between the person and his or her own *'pattern of meaningful relations in which a person exists and in the design of which he or she participates'*.[23] Emphasizing the risk that is required of the person in initiating a creative act, May focuses upon the inescapable anxiety that such risk provoke. This anxiety is not merely focused upon the outcome, or product, of the act and the artist's or the world's judgement of it. Rather, May is far more concerned with the anxiety engendered in the process of the act itself which is fundamentally revelatory and thus capable of breaking down not only one's previously held conceptions and values, but also one's constructed identity.[24]

This last point suggests that artistic activity may well provide a means whereby the sedimentations and dissociations in the experienced self-structure become open to challenge (if only temporarily) so that novel, and more 'liberating', self/world interrelations are experienced by the artist. (This might be the basis to artists' oft-repeated statements that they feel themselves to be more 'real' when they are immersed in creative activity.) In a recent review of Elaine Scarry's text *On Beauty and Being Just*,[25] Stuart Hampshire summarizes Scarry's argument that *'Beauty, and the experience of it, "decenters" us . . . When we come upon beautiful things . . . we find that we are standing in a different relation to the world than we were a moment before.'*[26] Indeed, according to Scarry, *'it is as though beautiful things have been placed here and there throughout the world to serve as small wake-up calls to perception, spurring lapsed alertness back to its most acute level'*.[27] I suggest that were we to replace the word *Beauty* with

Art, the worth of Scarry's (and Hampshire's) insights would not be compromised.

Such views remind us that our encounters with art provoke a somatically felt experience: through the shudder that courses through our bodies, the tingling that makes our hair stand on end, the tears we shed in wonder, the intake of breath. Experiences of this sort move us beyond the ordinary, beyond concepts and categories. Echoing this, George Steiner argues in his book *Real Presences*[28] that in our age art has become the single means left to us to catch a glimmer of transcendence. Our encounter with art, he asserts, '*is touched by the fear and ice of God*'.[29] This view once again resonates with Elaine Scarry's analysis of beauty:

> it sometimes seems that a special problem arises for beauty once the realm of the sacred is no longer believed in or aspired to. If a beautiful young girl . . . or a small bird, or a glass vase, or a poem, or a tree has the metaphysical . . . behind it, that realm verifies the weight and attention we confer on the girl, bird, vase, poem, tree. But if the metaphysical realm has vanished, one may feel bereft not only because of the giant deficit left by that vacant realm but because the girl, the bird, the vase, the book now seem unable in their solitude to account for the weight of their own beauty. If each calls out for attention that has no destination beyond itself, each seems self-centred, too fragile to support the gravity of our immense regard.[30]

I can think of no more direct or astute statement that so perfectly captures both the vital importance and current transcendental emptiness of art in our present culture. Much of the force that has provoked that self-centred, and arrogant, denial of the transcendent has its origins, and is maintained by, psychoanalytic theory in its many forms and derivations. That it has provided us with novel and important ways with which to look at ourselves is undeniable. However, in its unquestioning 'centredness' upon the intrapsychic and the conflicts and discontents that are claimed to arise therein, it has provoked world relations that must also remain focused upon, and can only be understood as extensions of, this internalized structure. The consequences of this catastrophic stance are most discernible in our attempts at, and relations towards, artistic creativity. And, I believe, it is necessary to ask in what ways has psychoanalysis assisted, however inadvertently, in promoting such extreme expressions of individualistic posturings and put-downs as have come to dominate current artistic expression in our culture?

In our ever more pervasive adoption of a stance towards the creative which has lost or forsaken its *real presences*, our experience of being human is not only impoverished, we *had* become less able to face up to its delight and anguish. While works of artistic creativity cannot provoke the delight or remove the anguish of our directly lived encounters with other human beings, they can, importantly, place these within an interrelational context with those other human qualities of fortitude and acceptance. I am reminded here of a beautiful scene in Woody Allen's *Manhattan* when the principal character reveals 'God's answer to Job'. Job asks: 'Lord, why do you put me through so much suffering?' God 'answers' him by pointing out the wonder and mystery of creation, and, faced with such, Job can only accept and persevere with what is placed before him.[31]

Existential phenomenology provides us with a means to articulate, and thereby reveal, both the rational and the somatically felt biases and limitations raised by the dominant cultural reliance upon, and allegiance to, psychoanalytic theories of artistic creativity. Further, in its pivotal challenge to the unsparing assertiveness of the individualistic psyche both in general and in the specific arena of artistic creativity, it can suggest other interrelational possibilities. Its insights point out to us that the act of creation has a momentum of its own. It is an act which distances the creative person from his or her day-to-day living and its concomitant problems and commitments, and, by doing so, permits the possibility of experiencing an aspect of being that is not usually – or ever – accessed elsewhere. Creativity contains strong elements of the mysterious and the unexpected. Even when the artist's end goal is clear, various novel routes, events and possibilities emerge seemingly out of nowhere, yet whose potential impact can alter the whole aim, goal, meaning or resolution of the work. And, just as significantly, those who make up the audience for an act of creation share some degree of this plunge into a transcendent unknown. Their relationship with the work also permits their 'truths' to emerge, and confront and transform.

While it must be admitted that the existential alternative for our understanding and appreciation of artistic creativity is, at present, 'a voice crying in the wilderness', it thankfully remains a voice none the less.

9 Beyond the great beyond

A couple of years ago, a client of mine, Paula, began our session somewhat uncharacteristically by recounting a dream she had had the night before. In that dream, she had felt herself to be witness to an odd encounter between myself and another, unnamed, female client. My dream client was a young Asian woman who appeared to be in great distress. Paula explained that it was obvious to her that the young woman was either on the verge of, or had just attempted, an act of suicide and that it had been due only to my sudden presence and calming influence that the act had either been put off or had failed. Paula was able to describe my Asian client's appearance in great detail, and was also able to delineate my own looks and clothing and, from these, deduct that, in the dream, I was a somewhat younger man, perhaps ten or fifteen years less than my actual age.

As well as this, Paula detailed a specific scene wherein she saw my client offer me a perfectly shaped and delicious-looking orange which, much to Paula's surprise, I somewhat brusquely rejected. Although Paula witnessed the scene as if she were watching a silent film, she could note the sudden look of utter dejection in my client's face, her blush of embarrassment or shame, the sudden rush of tears. Furthermore, still unable to hear what was being said, Paula explained that she could see me begin to speak and that my words must have soothed my client since her crying ceased and, in its place, she produced a resplendent smile. At that point, Paula became convinced that my Asian client was out of danger, that somehow I had succeeded in pulling her away from death's embrace.

Paula's dream had ended at that point and she had awakened experiencing a mixture of relief for my client and an overwhelming sense of sadness for herself. Towards me, or more accurately, towards the younger version of me who had appeared in the dream, she felt a confusion of anger and respect. But, Paula now asked, what did the dream mean? She could make no connection with the dream's participants and, in fact, felt herself to have been something of a 'dream voyeur' or, if not that, at least as someone who, in some mysterious fashion, had found herself dreaming someone else's dream.

This last comment by Paula, while not quite correct, was not entirely off the mark. What Paula did not (could not?) know was that the incident she had just described in such clear detail had not, for me at least, been a dream at all but rather was a substantially accurate retelling of an actual event that had taken place about eleven years earlier. At that time, I had been the therapist of a young Asian woman who had, in fact, made a half-hearted but none the less potentially successful attempt at suicide. She had phoned me at my home to inform me of what she had just done and I had been able to convince her to call an ambulance. The next morning I went to visit her, and in the course of our meeting she had offered me an orange which I had refused, owing to the strong allergic reaction that oranges provoke for me. As in the dream, my client's first reaction to my rejection of her gift had been one of upset. She had concluded incorrectly that my refusal indicated the anger I felt towards her for having forced me to cancel my engagements in order to visit her, and it was only when I was able to persuade her to listen to my disclosure regarding my allergy to oranges that she began to calm down and become convinced that I was there because I was concerned for her.

All this was odd enough; but odder events were to follow.

A few hours after Paula had left my home office, my telephone rang. When I picked it up, I was shocked to find that the caller was the very same Asian client whom I had not heard from nor spoken to for at least five years. She explained that she had decided to call on the spur of the moment because she had just peeled herself an orange and had suddenly been overwhelmed with memories of that morning after the night she had attempted suicide and had felt the need to speak to me again. What she wanted to tell me was that the combination of my having come to see her, and my openness about the effect of oranges upon me, had served to convince her that I genuinely cared about her and that, as a result, for the first time in a great many years, she had felt herself entitled to be loved by another human being. This realization was, for her, the key moment not only in our relationship with one another but, just as pertinently, in her relationship with herself and others in her world. We spoke for a few minutes longer, then she thanked me once again and said goodbye.

Needless to say, such incidents are not common in my life; I was, to put it mildly, shaken by this sequence of events. What is one to make of such an occurrence? Coincidence? Possibly. But there exist alternate, if more disconcerting, explanations, of course.

I am not, by any means, the only psychotherapist to have been confronted with potentially telepathic instances of this sort. Sigmund Freud himself wrote several papers on the topic of experiences of the uncanny during psychoanalysis,[1] and, while accepting the validity of telepathic phenomena, nevertheless insisted that analysts should not be side-tracked by their occurrence since to do so would keep the focus of analysis upon the surface, or manifest, level of experience rather than maintaining attention upon the exposure of their more hidden, or latent, source material.

In contrast to this stance, Freud's great rival, Carl Gustav Jung, hypothesized that these phenomena were direct

expressions of *the collective unconscious* (the psychic reposi-
tory of all the innate patterns of experience universally shared
by the human species). Together with the physicist, Wolfgang
Pauli, Jung coined the term *synchronicity* as a means of
expressing what he believed to be an acausal meaning connecting system of which telepathy was one of its
manifestations.[2]

Further, as was discussed in a recent paper read at the 1999
Annual Conference of the Transpersonal Psychology Section
of the British Psychological Society, many psychotherapists
report instances of 'transpersonal communication' with their
clients. More to the point, perhaps, both psychotherapists and
their clients tend to view these experiences as being special
and as catalysts to significant curative movement in the
therapy.[3]

I was myself an active researcher in various forms of what
might broadly be termed *paranormal phenomena* between the
years 1973 and 1982. The great majority of my research was
with children aged between 3 and 12 and was designed to test
the hypothesis that, under normal circumstances, instances of
phenomena such as those that have been commonly referred
to as *telepathy* decline in relation to human beings' increasing
ability to generate higher order cognitive functions. Summarizing its points very generally, my research considered the idea
that once a child develops that degree of cognitive functioning
wherein he or she becomes capable of internalizing and indi-
viduating *meaning connections*, his or her ability to produce
evidence of paranormal cognition will decline to the extent
that little, if any, evidence of it will emerge in controlled
studies. Since, in our culture, this level of cognitive development can usually be observed at around eight years of age,
subjects from this chronological age and upward should not,
in everyday conditions, demonstrate evidence of paranormal
cognition at levels other than what would be expected by
chance alone. Younger subjects, on the other hand, should be

able to do so at above-chance statistical levels. Or, to put it more simply, the younger the subjects' chronological age, the higher should be their ability to demonstrate paranormal cognition.

The data obtained from my studies strongly confirmed this hypothesis under several experimental conditions.[4] None the less, while these studies succeeded in convincing me, and a great many other researchers, that paranormal phenomena can be elicited even within the rigid and unusual conditions of a structured experiment, they have not yet been sufficiently replicated by other independent studies and, as such, cannot be said to provide conclusive scientific evidence – a common recurrence in just about every attempt to study paranormal phenomena under experimentally controlled conditions.

Acknowledging this, and, equally, admitting that what follows is entirely speculative, let me state what I believe to be (on the basis of reported studies on telepathy) the most likely conditions under which these kinds of phenomena will be manifested:

1 In highly emotional or disturbing conditions, such as in moments of life-threatening danger, or upon the moment of one's own death or the death of someone considered to be close to an individual such as a parent, child, sibling, spouse or friend.

2 Among subjects who exhibit some form of disabling psychological disorder or dysfunction – be it temporary or permanent.

3 In moments of deep relaxation – either by means of some technique such as a form of meditation, or, indeed, in moments of extreme boredom.

4 While dreaming, or under the conditions of hypnosis, trance states, focused prayer, drug-induced transcendental or psychedelic states, or during periods of extended alpha-wave brain activity.

5 Within cultures that rely upon 'group awareness' far more than do Western cultures for their members' continuing survival.
6 During periods of high arousal such as might occur during periods of highly concentrated creative, sexual or exploratory activity.
7 While in significant empathic contact with another.[5]

I find it interesting to note that the majority of these conditions present themselves during the process of psychotherapy and, as such, might shed some light as to why they appear to be reported by a wide range of psychotherapists. Yet, still the question remains: Why should they occur at all?

What I would argue is that a common feature of all the above instances is the disruption, or *plastification*, of one's self-consciousness and self-structure such that, in ways akin to the child studies discussed above, the selective filtering and protective barrier activities of the brain are temporarily disturbed or diminished.

As I argued in Chapter 1, a characteristic feature of *being human* lies in our recognition of, and attempts to deal with, various 'existence tensions' that are usually perceived as aspects of *opposition* such as life/death, directed activity/open passivity, stability/instability, certitude/incertitude, and so forth. Among these aspects, perhaps as a crucial factor of being human is that tension which can be expressed in terms of our desire to both assert our uniqueness and individuality and to 'fit into' a greater, or common, whole shared by all members of our species, if not all living organisms.

While human creations such as religion, political parties, specialist groups and affiliations, not to mention marriage and families, serve as commonly lived expressions of the human desire to 'belong', so, too, do instances of individual assertion in goal-directed behaviour, competitive and creative activities and physical appearance, as well as a plethora of overall identity characteristics, allow us to present ourselves as unique individuals who stand out in some way from all others.

However, while I have employed the term 'opposition' in order to convey my idea, I must qualify this to some degree. For, while such tendencies may well be typically perceived by many human beings as 'forces of opposition', phenomenologically derived consideration quickly clarifies that the assumption of opposition is somewhat misguided in that these tendencies reveal themselves to be *complementary* rather than oppositional and, on a wider plain of perspective, can be aligned to the broader notion of *figure/ground* in that each requires the other, and, indeed, exists only via its relation to the other.[6]

This brings me once more to the issue of 'self'. As far as we know, human beings have evolved in such a way that our ability to experience and express what has been termed *self-consciousness* far outstrips in its complexity that of every other animal. While we have understood very little of the aetiology, functions and neurophysiological basis of self-consciousness at a theoretical level,[7] it remains evident that at the immediately-lived level the vagaries of the self are all too obvious.

As I discussed in Chapter 3, existential phenomenology places us in a fundamental *with-world*, or *interrelational* context through which all meaningful reflections upon our existence emerge. In doing so, 'the self' is perceived to be a constructed product or outcome of reflective activity rather than its initiator. Considered in this light, 'the self' exists as a product of *between relations* rather than residing 'within' a being and, as an interrelational construct, is far more plastic and complex than many other Western theories would typically have us suppose. From my work as a psychotherapist, for instance, much of my engagement with clients examines and challenges assumptions they hold about 'real and false' selves, multiple and dissociated selves and the like. In this way, self/ other, like figure/ground, expresses complementary rather than oppositional characteristics.[8]

While very little is known about the nature of self-consciousness, not least at what stage in our development this particular expression of consciousness emerges, the chronological range for its initial formation presented by theorists typically encompasses the period between embryological fertilization and age 3.[9] Nevertheless, whenever it may be that self-consciousness becomes possible, it seems reasonable to suggest, on the basis of wider studies on child development, that a relatively fixed sense of self will take some time to become coherent to us and that, for some period throughout our infancy and childhood, our explorations of the boundaries of self, and our ability to distinguish self from others or 'other selves', requires sufficient accumulation of experience as well as various neurophysiological developments.[10] If so, then an earlier, more 'plastic' sense of self-structure and boundary may well be expressed in a greater tendency to 'intrude upon' or 'share' meaningful input that might otherwise be assumed to reside within other 'selves'. If, as phenomenological theorists have suggested, our self-consciousness is an interrelational product, it remains possible to speculate that in its early stages of existence self-consciousness remains at a relatively 'unboundaried', or plastic, level, such that it may extend beyond the separate confines of one biological being to encompass, at least in part, and temporarily, the self-consciousness of one or more other beings.

An obvious example of this phenomenon might be the symbiotic relationship that has been noted to exist between mothers and their infant children. The psychoanalyst Jan Ehrenwald, for instance, argued that in the early post-partum phase, the mother's and the neonate's ego boundaries have not yet been delineated such that their respective egos are merged in a physiologically reciprocal beneficial relationship which, at times, reveals itself in ways that express themselves via non-sensory (i.e. paranormal) cues.[11]

Perhaps equally relevant, if far wider in its speculative implications, is Whately Carington's hypothesis of consciousness which, he suggests, does not reside 'within' any individual but rather, insofar as it might have a location, exists *around* or *between* beings and is given expression as self-consciousness through the relational interaction between this consciousness field and the individual being's brain.[12] In this way, consciousness is seen as being neither an expression nor a product of brain activity, nor can it be said to 'reside within' a brain. Rather, it is more akin to a non-localized energy field that interacts with the brain in much the same fashion as would be hypothesized by field theory in modern physics.

A significant corollary of this hypothesis would suggest that the primary function of the human brain becomes not that of *generating* consciousness but, rather, that of serving as a *selective filter* of consciousness. This idea of the brain as selective filter is anything but far-fetched. Countless psychological studies on attention, for instance, reveal the brain's necessary task of selectively restricting the near infinite quantity of incoming data from awareness.[13] I would suggest that it might also be the case that, for those beings who have developed a specific, individual, self-consciousness, the brain must evolve so that it also acts as a barrier that protects those aspects of consciousness allied to 'self' against general diffusion and availability to other 'selves'.

I would put forward this possibility as a plausible explanation for the appearance of paranormal phenomena whether under the more general set of conditions summarized above or under the specific conditions and focus of my own research studies. With regard to the latter, what I am suggesting is that in not having as yet fully developed a clear and relatively fixed sense of 'self', the filtering and barrier-like functions of my younger subjects' brains were not fully operational such that these subjects were better able to 'share' the relational input generated by the interaction between brain and consciousness. While noting from the outset that the uncanny account with which I opened this chapter may well have contained several of these elements, let me return to it for further analysis.

My sessions with Paula, whom I had been seeing for over two years, had reached a crisis of sorts. We had done good work together, and she had found the strength and courage to begin to deal with a number of recurring debilitating patterns in her life's relations both with herself and her husband, by whom she had felt betrayed as a result of her discovery of his long-term ongoing affair with one of his colleagues. In the weeks leading up to her recounting of the dream, Paula had begun to consider ending therapy since, as she saw it, she and her husband had found the means with which to regain a meaningful sense of reconnection with one another that, they both believed, would sustain their marriage. In response, I had expressed my willingness to assist Paula in working through the ending of our therapy, if that was what she wanted. She thanked me for not making any attempt to dissuade her from her decision and asserted that she would think further about the issue before arriving at a decision. Indeed, she continued to remind me at the start of each subsequent session that 'she was still thinking about what she would do'.

During the session following her 'inexplicable dream', Paula admitted that the dream had continued to bother her, not least because, try as she might, she still could not make sense of it. We agreed to discuss it further and began by summarizing it once again. During the course of this exercise, our discussion began to focus upon my relationship with my dream client, how I had been concerned about her, and had expressed my care for her by 'breaking various psychotherapeutic boundaries' by visiting her in hospital. Eventually, the theme of my expression of concern and care for my dream client began to dominate our dialogue until, much to my initial amazement (and as a consequence of my obvious stupidity!), Paula became increasingly agitated and angry with me.

Finally giving full vent to her feelings, Paula began to scream at me. Couldn't I see how envious she felt about the way I was with my dream client? Was it not obvious to me that she – Paula – might be asking herself why it should be that I could so easily express my care and concern towards my dream client while, towards her, I had shown no sign of anything approaching something similar? And had I not made that blatantly obvious to her by not responding at all to her threat to terminate psychotherapy? Did she really mean so little to me?

Taken aback as I was, I could now see that, albeit in uncanny fashion, Paula's dream had managed to encapsulate and give expression to her feelings of not being cared for by me in a most direct yet still self-protective way. For, in recounting this particular dream she had been able to convey the kind of relationship that she desired to have with me while, at the same time, by taking herself out of the dream (and becoming a detached observer) she could indicate her desire via my dream client, thereby avoiding the full brunt of potentially hurtful consequences that could still arise were I to reveal to her that, in truth, I felt neither care nor concern for her.

What she remained unaware of, of course, was that the dream images held additional resonance for me in that they bore striking similarities with actual past events. Furthermore, as if her 'message' to me had not been sufficiently conveyed via the dream, had not the remarkable telephone call I had received also sought to communicate the theme of 'care and concern' once again?

Considered more generally, and adopting an existential-phenomenological perspective, events like this can be considered as instances of dialogical engagement that for diverse reasons, be they circumstantial or purposefully planned, shift individuals away – whether willingly or unwillingly – from more securely defined and bounded perspectives of 'self' towards those co-constituted or *life-world* reflections which permit – or impose – a temporary attunement towards far less boundaried self/world interrelations.

None the less, while, via the dream, Paula and I were now able to address the issues between us and, in this fashion (and, as well, in recognition of what a dullard I can be at times) we began to find the means whereby the previously minimally expressed human dimensions in our continuing encounters became more overtly acknowledged.

All well and good; but various disturbing questions remain unanswered. For, no matter the attempted solution put forward, and even if this solution might be shown to be of some clarificatory value, the specificity and complexity of the confluent variables that make up this uncanny account are nothing less than mind-boggling in their defiance of what might be deemed to be a 'reasonable' explanation for their occurrence.

This last point leads me to a broader concern. Just as it is patently obvious that paranormal experiences continue to fascinate and disturb most – if not all – of us in the West, irrespective of whether we classify ourselves as believers or sceptics with regard to these phenomena, it remains necessary to ask ourselves what it is about these self-same phenomena that so intrigues us. One response is that we are simply interested in the possibilities and limitations of human consciousness, but I doubt that this is the most likely answer.

Rather, if we examine the rise of this fascination in the West over the past century or so, we are bound to note that its principal impetus lay in the search for evidence for survival of personality after death.[14] It is this fundamental concern, the anxiety it generates for us and the possibility of its alleviation, that, I believe, spurs much of our continuing fascination with paranormal phenomena.

While I write as one who considers the seemingly endless

speculation on this matter to be at best, irrelevant, and at worst a serious impediment to the possibilities of living available to us, nevertheless, I would be foolish (and worse!) were I to avoid acknowledging the persisting conundrums provoked for us by the spiritual and religious beliefs we may uphold or deny. Such concerns and how they come to be expressed by us tell us, at least in part, a great deal about our stance and attitude towards death.

In line with many other authors on the subject, the existential psychotherapist, Rollo May, has suggested that the issue of death encompasses contemporary Western society's greatest taboo.[15] Just as we have, with ever greater insistence, learned to avoid the acknowledgement of death in any number of ways, not least by employing euphemistic terms such as 'passed on' or 'gone away', so, too, have we elevated *the cult of youth* to such an extent that any product or surgical intervention designed to provide the illusory appearance of youthfulness is eagerly sought after by a great many of those whose physical appearance betrays the fact of their natural ageing. Increasingly, the older (-looking) citizen in our society has come to be identified primarily as an ambassador of death and so is shunned, dismissed and diminished as a human being.

Further, the expansion of an increasingly dehumanizing technological treatment of those among the aged who are either terminally ill or dying has robbed us all of crucial emotional and interpersonal experiences that not only permit the experience of grief but which also, paradoxically, can provide us with a fundamental sense of life's worth and wonder. This expulsion of death as an inherent feature of life appears to have as its impetus the attempt to avoid all confrontation with mystery; it is our effort to eradicate the fear of the unknown.

In a society that emphasizes an ever more exciting, productive and meaningful 'tomorrow', any reminders of the possibility that there may not be a tomorrow are to be avoided at all costs. And if such cannot be so easily avoided? Then the conviction that there may still exist a non-material, spiritual tomorrow becomes that much more appealing . . . and necessary. Such convictions are not, of course, new either to this society or to humankind as a whole. Our awareness of our mortality is a distinct feature of our species – as is our tendency to speculate upon an afterlife.

Personally, I distrust any statement that asserts either the endurance, or its impossibility, of an existence beyond death. Instead, I share the sentiments expressed by Arthur Koestler in the note he wrote immediately prior to his suicide:

> **I wish my friends to know that I am leaving their company . . . with some timid hopes for a depersonalised after-life beyond due confines of space, time and matter and beyond the limits of our comprehension. This 'oceanic feeling' has often sustained me at difficult moments, and does so now, while I am writing this.**[16]

What I take from Koestler's words is the acknowledgement of the unknown (and possibly the unknowable) that infuses our lives. Some may prefer to label this impenetrable possibility 'god'. For me, the term is too loaded, too infused with our human attempts to fashion our gods in our own image and to equip them with qualities and frailties, attitudes and judgements that remain all too limited and limiting in their human dimensions. The existential philosopher Jean-Paul Sartre may well have been correct to insist that our project as human beings is to become god.[17] But, if so, the critical enterprise in our project is that of obliterating the unknown, of achieving absolute certainty over all and everything.

Yet, via our advances in science and technology, as we more ever closer towards the fulfilment of our project, as we approach our human version of 'godhood', what we appear to be losing is our very humanity. If it is the case that death makes life meaningful, it may also be worth considering that the acknowledgement of the unknown in our lives provides an opening, a possibility of the unforeseen and unexpected in all that which appears to be known to us – whether it be ourself, others or the world in general and all the interrelational possibilities that exist between them.

Faced with such, how might we best respond to those instances which point us towards some possible 'beyond'? I suggest the following: A smile. A shudder. A shrug of resignation . . . and acceptance.

10 The mirror and the hammer: some hesitant steps towards a more humane psychotherapy

Unlike many of my colleagues, I have never considered psychotherapy to be 'my calling'. I cannot remember a time in my youth when, faced with considering the various work options open to me, I gave psychotherapy any serious thought. It was, more accurately, a profession into which I somehow drifted more out of unforeseen circumstance than planned action. Still, I would not deny that a number of the themes and issues surrounding psychotherapy interested me, and, happily, continue to do so. Nonetheless, while I mainly enjoy and value my encounters with clients, students and colleagues, it remains the case that I can conjure up other areas of interest and enjoyment that equal, if not surpass, the stimulation and pleasure provided me by psychotherapy.

Although I remain an active, if often critical, exponent of the values and benefits of psychotherapeutic encounters in that I both practise psychotherapy and make attempts to train others to become psychotherapists, I must confess that my own experiences of being in psychotherapy as a client have been on the whole disappointing with regard both to the quantity and quality of insights they have provoked. Indeed, to speak more plainly, that with which psychotherapy has provided me as a client has been minimal when compared to any number of other exploratory activities in which I have engaged throughout my life. When placed next to my experiences of visiting and living in foreign countries, of sociopolitical involvement, of reading and writing fiction and poetry, of meditation, of immersion in music and song, of recording and exploring my dreams or watching others' dreams projected on to cinema screens or canvases or chiselled out of rock, and, most of all, of allowing myself to feel love for others and to feel another's love for me, that which I have gained from my personal therapy remains barely significant.

In disclosing this, I do not wish to leave readers with the false impression that, somewhat cynically, I have judged psychotherapy to offer little of worth other than as a means to some degree of personal financial security. Only that my encounters as a client with *my* own therapists have lacked what I can only call that vital 'human' dimension, that 'honest and open meeting of beings' that infuses anything which illuminates and brings meaning to one's life. This is what I have sought to offer to my clients and students and which I have been blessed in receiving through my ongoing encounters with them. I can only hope that they have experienced something similar in their encounters with me.

I am by no means the first, and will in all likelihood not be the last, to give voice to these views. Indeed, in recent years there has been a groundswell of written accounts both by psychotherapists and clients expressing a wide range of critical views and concerns surrounding the practice of psychotherapy.[1]

In the great majority of such instances the voices raised have been disparaging of any number of theory-derived stances and techniques adopted by psychotherapists in their interactions with clients. A recent book by Anna Sands, *Falling For Therapy: Psychotherapy From a Client's Point of View*, is, in many ways, typical of this tendency. Throughout her account, Sands takes issue with a number of interrelational attitudes, such as psychotherapists' insistence upon their own personal privacy or anonymity, their transformation of her criticisms as manifestations of 'transference' and the like, as being questionable, limiting, contradictory and potentially harmful stances for them to take towards her and, by implication, all of their clients. Further, she suggests that these stances, as well as being deeply confusing to the client, serve to dehumanize the relationship and benefit only the imbalances of power in their relations and the perpetuation of the mystique of psychotherapy.[2]

While I generally share Ms Sands' concerns, as an 'insider', I can also assess, perhaps more accurately than she, the limited impact of these critiques. For, when confronted with such, the response of many psychotherapists is likely to be: 'But she has not understood the need for us to maintain these uncommon attitudes and dispositions if there is to be any hope for the therapy to fulfil its ameliorative possibilities. The psychotherapeutic relationship is like no other and, as such, requires particular forms of intercourse and intervention – no matter how unusual or unacceptable these might be in other types of social interaction.'

Although I am not convinced by such reasoning, let me suppose, for the sake of argument, that they are, in essence, correct at least insofar as they are the necessary underpinnings of a particular, and currently dominant, view of psychotherapy. Let me also concede that this view permits both 'fundamentalist' and 'liberal' interpretations of these necessary underpinnings – of which existential psychotherapy may be its most liberal proponent.

What I want to consider in this chapter, however haltingly (for, on the whole, I consider my own practice to be well within the boundaries of 'liberalism'), is a more radical proposal. In doing so, I am at least in part aware that the views I will put forward may appear to many of my readers to threaten the very possibility of the therapeutic enterprise. As a consequence, I may well be judged as being arrogant, naive and irresponsible or, worse, my very credentials as a psychotherapist may be called into question by at least some of my colleagues. If so, I suppose I will be placed within a particular circle of disgruntled individuals and, like them, become labelled as one more among the numerous cranks (and the occasional visionaries cohabiting a nearby terrain) who have railed against the parameters of this strange profession.

At about the same time that I read Anna Sands' book, I chanced upon an advertisement for a memoir by Emily Fox Gordon entitled *Mockingbird Years: A Life In and Out of Therapy.*[3] My first reaction to it was to suppose that it would be yet another in a developing category of psychotherapeutically focused texts written by ex-clients: the '*read how psychotherapy messed me up and how awful (or evil) it is*' genre. I have read a number of these books and have even contributed an Afterword to one.[4] However, while I champion the courage of their authors, and usually sympathize with the iniquities thrown their way under the guise of theory or technique, I must confess that I have gained little insight from them and, in common with other colleagues' reading of such texts, I have tended to conclude (quite conceitedly, I accept) something like: '*But I and my way of working are nothing like what is being described*, and to move on to something more challenging.

None the less, for reasons I have yet to ascertain, I experienced an urgent desire to read Ms Gordon's text and duly ordered it. Having done so, I can state in all honesty that, for me, this was one of those key texts that succeed in provoking a sense of disturbing recognition of their having captured something felt but for which no adequate words to give expression to that feeling had been found – until now.

Gordon's memoir recounts various meetings with a series of unremarkable men and women who had been her psychotherapists. Interweaved with these often hilarious and harrowing vignettes she writes about incidents in her life with her parents, her friends, her relationship with her husband, and her encounters with institutionalized colleagues who, like her, were forced to 'put up with' the inadequate interventions of those who sought to 'make her better'. As a counterpoint to the negligible impact of other psychotherapists, Gordon discusses her encounters with Dr Leslie Farber – an altogether different kind of psychotherapist.

Although Farber was a respected psychoanalyst and author of a number of highly regarded papers published in specialist journals and textbooks, it is quickly made apparent that he was highly critical of the psychotherapeutic enterprise as understood by his peers and that his way of working with his clients was, to put it mildly, unorthodox.

Gordon writes that Farber, who greatly admired the writings of the Danish philosopher Søren Kierkegaard, considered psychotherapists to be

> like a man who has spent decades building a splendid mansion, a great multistoried edifice with wings flung out in every direction. But when the man has finally completed his dream house, he settles contentedly into a shack next door. In Dr Farber's view, the house of psychoanalysis was impressive but unfit for human habitation.[5]

Gordon tells us:

> I knew instantly that Dr Farber was a different kind of being from other therapists. His was not the neutral watchfulness I had become so used to; he judged, and revealed his judgement . . . I also sensed, if obscurely, that he was a person whose way of looking at the world . . . was integrated with, and undetachable from, his self.[6]

For Farber, the experience of engaging in psychotherapy was inseparable from that of being in a friendship. His stance was focused upon a moral, rather than a technique-dominated, and hence safer, professional engagement with his clients. One obvious way of gaining a sense of what Gordon is seeking to convey about Farber's stance can be gleaned from what she tells us of their discussions:

> **What did we talk about? We talked of Dr Farber's childhood . . . We talked about my childhood . . . We talked about his marriages and my boyfriends. We talked about his growing despair at watching . . . patients . . . loitering in a psychiatric limbo . . . We talked about the youth culture . . . We talked about movies and TV.**[7]

Just from this brief extract, we can begin to understand that Farber found little value in the maintenance of a psychotherapeutic neutrality and anonymity. But this is but the tip of the iceberg. Soon enough, Gordon reveals that Farber was willing to meet her as often she wished (so long as he was free to do so) and that their sessions could be brief or extend far beyond the 'magical' fifty minutes. Further, Farber saw no reason to limit such meetings to his office, and instead was willing to go out on walks with her, introduce her to his family, invite her to his home, and provide her with meals and informal, unboundaried, discussion. As far as one can tell, Farber did not do this because he had singled out Gordon as being someone 'special' or requiring unusual degrees of psychotherapeutic attention; instead, this stance towards Gordon was not untypical of his wider stance towards each of his clients. In similar fashion, Farber did not ask or demand anything in particular from Gordon other than she treat him with a similar kind of human respect and dignity that he sought to embody in his relations with her. As Gordon explains:

> **In his practice with patients, Dr Farber was both far humbler than his more conventional colleagues and far bolder: He was humbler because he approached his patients as a whole human being, not as a semianonymous representative of his profession,**

> and because he had abandoned his profession's claims to
> objectivity and curative power. He was bolder because when he
> took on a patient, he committed himself to a risky, open-ended
> friendship and to all the claims of responsibility that friendship
> entails. It was a brave venture to step from behind the mask of
> his profession, and a dangerous one . . . Many other
> psychotherapists did something similar in the 1960s, of course,
> often with disastrous results.[8]

What was different about Farber in this last, distinguishing respect was that he seemed to be well aware of the interrelational responsibilities that are required if one is to venture into such perilous territories. '*He was toughminded, and he held himself very carefully in check. His boundaries were moral, not professional. They were part of his being – not a stifling suit of armor but a flexible skin.*'[9]

I would not be surprised if, by this point, the reader may have begun to experience conflicting attitudes towards Farber's 'way of being a psychotherapist'. While there may be some sense of attraction towards Farber's humane attitude in his relations with his clients, there is also likely to be an opposite, niggling concern that his stance breaks all the rules of contemporary psychotherapy. To her credit, Gordon is equally clear-sighted and concludes that '*I can well understand how . . . any mainstream psychotherapist . . . would have no choice but to judge Farber guilty of serious malpractice.*'[10]

But then, in response to her (and our) concerns she challenges her readers with an equally disturbing question: *So what?*

> If Dr Farber's aim had been solely or even principally a
> therapeutic one, the criticisms . . . would have been
> germane . . . [I]n the name of therapy, Farber was doing
> something quite different. His aim . . . was a radical departure
> from the ordinary goal of therapy: He meant to offer hope to his

> patients through talk. This was not talk that centered,
> necessarily, around their problems – it was just the best and
> most honest talk that he and they were capable of. He meant to
> break the logic of despair, and his goal in doing so was not a
> primarily therapeutic one . . . [T]he aim was not so much to
> restore the patient's health as it was to free him from illusion
> . . . [A]lthough his worldview was tragic, truth was transcendent,
> and always held a possibility of hope.[11]

It would seem to me that what Gordon is expressing through these statements is that Farber had shifted the enterprise of psychotherapy away from a set of methodological conditions and, instead, was attempting to replace these with an attitude that expressed a way of being with others that paralleled his broader, more general way of being with self and the world. He did not merely 'do' psychotherapy; rather his way of being a psychotherapist could not be separated from his way of being human.

Thus far, I have read only one paper by Farber,[12] but if this paper is representative of his wider range of writing, I believe his work has been unjustly neglected by contemporary psychotherapy. He deserves much more attention and consideration and there is a great deal to be learned from him.

Farber, who placed so much import on language and discourse, was unhesitantly critical of the language of psychotherapy in general and, in particular, of the way that even the most human-focused psychotherapists chose to write about their clients.

> The people are written about as if they are 'creatures . . . [who]
> . . . may bear some resemblance to animals, or to steam
> engines or robots or electronic brains, they do not sound like
> people. They are in fact constructs of theory, more humanoid
> than human; and whether they are based on the libido theory or
> on the new inter-personal theories of relationships, it is just

> **those qualities most distinctively human which seem to have been omitted.**[13]

He argued that it is quite a different matter to ask 'What is man?' as opposed to 'What is it to be human?' The former question forces us towards abstraction, removes us from a shared realm of mutual experience and places us in the terrain of clinically detached observation and conceptualization. This, for him, was the path adopted and advocated by his colleagues. His way, instead, argued for a quite different approach to the understanding of, and meeting with, one's clients.

> **Obviously, if meeting is to occur in psychotherapy, it will occur**
> **_despite_ . . . inequalities in position, status, background,**
> **education or awareness. Within the therapeutic dialogue, the**
> **initiative, hopefully, is the therapist's. It is up to him whether he**
> **can forsake the academy in order to address his patient not as an**
> **object of knowledge, but as a being engaged in the task [as**
> **Kierkegaard puts it] of becoming 'what he is already: namely a**
> **human being.**[14]

Farber railed against the adoption of a conventional scientific prose that seeks to disguise, but cannot truly conceal, '_the pathos of two maddened human beings clutching at each other, whatever the pretext_'.[15]

When I first read this last sentence, I was both deeply shaken and confused. What on earth was Farber attempting to convey? If I have not misunderstood his words, I believe they seek to capture a crucial awareness which, among other things, paves the way for a radical departure from more ordinary understandings of the therapeutic relationship.

Farber argued that the benefits of a psychotherapeutic relationship begin to emerge only when the client ascertains that the relationship is mutually beneficial to both participants. These benefits emerge precisely when the client, through this understanding, and something akin to a concomitant concern (or 'pity', as Farber labels it) for the therapist, agrees to '*under-take therapeutic efforts which, although clearly beneficial to himself, have as their primary motive the assuaging of another's pain*'.[16] It is through the client's connection with the psychotherapist's own confusion and despair of being human, and hence the acceptance of the uncertainty and wonderment that expresses itself in every facet of his or her life (including, of course, that part of life that constitutes 'being and working as a psychotherapist'), that the client may find the will to recognize and respond in a compassionate fashion to the concern that infuses the therapist's way of being with another (the client).

For Farber, this critical choice on the part of the client to move out of his or her own exclusive and limited self-focused pattern of engagement and, instead, seek to embrace the world of the psychotherapist, serves to confirm the humanity of the participants both to themselves and to one another and, in turn, permits their encounter to be expressive of its human and humane qualities.

Farber suggests that this 'turn' on the part of the client provides the psychotherapist with the will to be the dedicated, even courageous, human being he or she is capable of being, and, in the same way, provokes the same felt qualities for the client. '*Pity demands an imagining of the other's particular pain to the degree that the pain is experienced as one's own. In therapy the paradox is inescapable that the man who is incapable of arousing pity will find it hard to help another.*'[17]

When I first began to glimpse the meaning of Farber's assertion, I was both flooded with a new-found understanding of the possibilities of psychotherapy and moved to tears. I could see that whatever 'success' I may have had through my therapeutic work with my clients came about not through my skilful interventions, nor even through such qualities of care and respect that I was able to muster forth in my relations with them, but, rather, had emerged through a *mutual* acceptance of our shared powerlessness and uncertainty in the face of the 'impossible dilemmas of being human'. And further, that paradoxically, via this very acceptance, both I and my clients discovered some well-spring of power that permitted us to disclose ourselves to, and be disclosed by, the presence of the other.

Many clients who have either benefited from, or, equally, have been damaged by, psychotherapy, have placed the psychotherapist's power, or more advanced (or elevated) way of being, as the source of their experience. While I have been willing to accept that this is what these clients have come to believe, knowing all too well my own and fellow psychotherapists' frailties and conflicting confusions regarding our own lives, I could not come to the same conclusion. But Farber has provided what is to me a far sounder alternative perspective. It may well be that in those instances when both client and psychotherapist turn towards the other and, not in spite of but *because* they permit themselves to ascertain the other's frailties and are willing to embrace them as their own, then, through this very act of human caring, each experiences that necessary empowerment to be, and to be seen to be, the being they both aspire to become. In similar fashion, it may well also be the case that when the client experiences the psychotherapist's authority and power as unhelpful or oppressive, this is an outcome of the psychotherapist's unwillingness to accept the client's frailties as belonging not just to the client alone. As such, no matter how concerned or caring he or she may be towards the client, the psychotherapist's unwillingness to stand revealed as human in turn prevents the possibility of the client's concern being directed towards another (the psychotherapist).

The person who most influenced Farber's approach to psychotherapy was the philosopher and Jewish theologian Martin Buber. Farber returns again and again to Buber's writings concerning what he called 'interhuman relations'.[18] Emily Fox Gordon provides an insightful summary of these views.

> **The interhuman is the 'life between person and person'. It is distinct from the social and collective realm. The interhuman is an end, not a means. It has no utility, it is not the foundation on which society is built, and it can be inimical to society's purposes. What happens in life between person and person can carry psychological and sociological meanings, of course, but these are incidental to the fact of meeting itself.[19]**

She argues that Farber's psychotherapeutic practice exemplified Buber's notion of interhuman relations. In particular, she suggests, Farber sought to demonstrate these qualities *'through talk, of how talk is to be treated not as a means to a therapeutic end but as the central source of moral meaning itself'*.[20] Unlike other psychotherapists who all rely upon 'talk' as their primary means towards ameliorative change, Farber understood, through his study of Buber, that talking cannot be turned into a technique or a 'cure'. For Farber, talk was not a means to a designated end; rather, it was an end in itself in that it was the very expression of interhuman relations. As such, his 'talks' with his clients could be, and were, as Gordon makes so plain, about anything. Their content did not truly matter. Rather, the talk between Farber and his clients served to illuminate the worth and possibilities of open, honest and 'care-full' human encounter.

Gordon writes:

> **In the offices of my earlier therapists, I had understood that the world was to be kept at bay; pieces of it entered the room as carefully prepared specimens ready for examination and analysis. But in Dr Farber's office, the world flowed in freely and surrounded us . . . [and] would take shape between us.[21]**

Farber had seen that interhuman relations require the acknowledgement of the world as their context. In recognizing this, he sought to welcome the world into the encounter between himself and his clients, sometimes through the subject matter of their talks (such as politics, cinema, social events), at others by quite deliberately engaging in talks with his clients outside the secluded confines of his office (in parks and city streets, at his home in the company of his family, with significant others in the client's wider world).

In chapters 1 and 2 of this book, I argued that while existential psychotherapy has implicitly acknowledged the contextualizing presence of the world within the therapeutic relationship, this stance could, perhaps should, be made far more explicit. I suggested that one important way by which this could be made more obvious was through the focus upon what I termed 'the they-focused' relations in the client's life. While this may be a sufficient means by which the world can be returned to the therapeutic encounter, Farber's example provides alternative, perhaps more straightforward, possibilities.

I realize that the great majority of my existential colleagues would consider it unacceptable, perhaps even potentially abusive, for them to engage in talk with their clients outside the confines of their offices. What would it mean to the client, and what disturbing impact might there be upon the relationship if, for instance, the talks took place outdoors, in public, or even (a dreadful possibility, this) in the client's home? What price might be paid in this calling forth of, and towards, the world?

In all honesty, I do not know. But if, as existential psychotherapists often claim, their approach stands as being the most sceptically enquiring of all psychotherapeutic stances and, as well, that they are in the forefront of the exploration of the intersubjective, then, surely we can be sufficiently free and responsible in addressing such questions? After all, Søren Kierkegaard, the philosopher whose writings most clearly anticipated the existential movement, urged his readers '*to say what you mean and to do what you say'*.[22] At times, it appears to me, existential psychotherapy, while being bold in 'saying what it means', may well have remained unnecessarily timid in considering what implications there may be in its 'doing what it says'.

Among the latter, surely, existential psychotherapy's continuing subservience to other psychotherapeutic models' – and, most significantly, the psychoanalytic model's – assumptions regarding the therapeutic necessity of keeping the world at bay via the exclusionary boundaries imposed and maintained behind the closed consulting room door requires the sort of open consideration that might lead to less secure alternatives?

Emily Fox Gordon's memoir concludes with what I believe to be one of the most pertinent critiques of contemporary psychotherapy. Taking Buber as her guide, she argues that:

> It was clear that when Buber was writing midcentury that a psychotherapeutic ethic was in the ascendancy, and that for this ethic to prevail, more and more that was heretofore accepted as part of the human condition, to be endured or celebrated or transcended . . . would be relegated to the realm of the pathological. There were benefits in this, of course – no sensible person could deny that therapy practiced as an art can be a force for good – but in the general progress of therapy, there was also a great and terrible loss of meaning. It was the realm of the interhuman that steadily shrank as therapy advanced . . . The world we live in now is one in which nearly all of us . . . are so thoroughly indoctrinated in the ideology of therapy that society has remade itself in therapy's image. To one degree or another, nearly every encounter looks like therapy now . . . If therapy is all that we can give, or receive, then the possibility of mutuality has all but vanished.[23]

Perhaps foolishly, perhaps because, notwithstanding my reservations, I have invested so much of my life in exploring the potential worth of psychotherapy, I cannot fully agree with her conclusion. In addition, because, while recognizing that I have found no argument with which to disprove her contention, I continue to disagree, I am obliged to consider radical alternatives such as those posed by Leslie Farber.

I confess, with some all too real trepidation, to having begun various cautious explorations along the lines suggested by him. I state this neither out of desire for fame (nor infamy) nor because I wish to enjoin others to follow either my or Farber's path. I initiated these gropings in the dark before my chance discovery of Farber's work through Gordon's account of her psychotherapy with him. And, while I have gained some further clarity (however potentially illusory) through this, I remain, at present, in no position to assert the worth of the enterprise. If anything, in fact, I am suffused with the dreadful concern that I may be profoundly in error and that, if so, it is not I alone, or even principally, who may suffer as a consequence.

Recently, I spoke of these matters to my friend and colleague Dr Bo Jacobsen, who is himself an existential psychotherapist practising and teaching in Copenhagen, Denmark (which, aptly, was Kierkegaard's 'home turf'). Bo's main comment to me is one I have taken to heart: 'What makes you so arrogant to suppose that you, on your own, have the right to attempt this?'

Once again, I have no answer except to note that while I mainly continue to experience what may well be the very opposite of arrogance, I remain determined not to shun its possibilities. Perhaps naively, I continue to believe that if the meeting point between human beings is approached with all the honesty and respect one can muster, and that those same qualities are shared by self and other, there will be no critical danger. 'Ah . . . But,' my colleagues will respond, 'how can you be certain that your clients *are* capable of these very qualities?' In all honesty, I know that I cannot be certain – either of them, or of myself. As a psychotherapist, I share the view that any worthwhile encounter requires *a leap of faith*, a living with uncertainty not only on the part of the client, but of the therapist as well. In the past, I have watched my clients take such leaps from a vantage point of relative security. And while, today, I feel no compulsion to ask anything more of them than that which they are already willing to undertake, I have begun to hear a somewhat insistent voice urging me to find something of their courage in my own stance. It remains to be seen whether this voice is the call of conscience or of hubris.

In asking myself how I might make some sense of my embrace of this uncertain and uneasy path, I am reminded that I have sometimes suggested – not entirely in jest – that the complex workings of existential psychotherapy might best be likened, at least to some degree, to a number of primary aspects of a model of contemporary physics that has become known as *chaos theory*.

Chaos theory arose due to the lack of success of previous, linearly derived, Euclidian models of physics in accurately understanding and predicting many types of complex, if naturally occurring, behaviours such as the turbulence of water coming out of a spout, or the flow of blood through the heart, or of the sudden, sometimes subtle, sometimes dramatic, changes in weather systems. Chaos theory argues that such behaviours are sensitively dependent upon any number of subtle changes in a complexity of variables (the so-called 'butterfly effect').[24]

Unlike the more regular, and, hence more straightforwardly predictable changes in motion and direction studied so exhaustively, and successfully, by classical physicists, the behaviour of complex systems, while clearly *not* random and unpredictable, none the less reveals often immensely subtle regularities that can only begin to be discerned when investigators cease seeking to place them within the confines of linearly causal analyses.

Since the behaviour of human beings falls into the category of 'complex systems', it would seem that something akin to chaos theory is required in order for a more adequate understanding of the possibilities and ramifications of psychotherapy to emerge. Yet it appears difficult for us to acknowledge this characteristic aspect of human existence. Typically, we in the West in particular, have allowed ourselves to be soothed by the deception that sudden change is something that occurs *outside the normal order of things*. Any significant change in circumstance or experience is perceived by us to be an exception to the rule, and not the rule itself. We find it awkward to conceive of the idea of sudden radical linearly irrational change as being a fundamental given of complex beings; yet this is precisely what chaos theory implies.

The revolutionary shift in thinking presented to us by chaos theory is a fundamental one to science. Since its formal inception some five hundred years ago, science has been about control and ultimately, total control, over everything. However, during the course of the twentieth century such a claim, at least when applied to complex systems, began to shatter.

Speaking personally, my attraction to this model lies in its ability to confirm that which in some way I had intuited about the shifting changes and movements in my own life. If I come to a point where I ask myself: 'How did I ever get to this particular "here"?', I am forced to conclude that no amount of linearly derived 'cause and effect explanation' begins to provide me with a remotely satisfactory solution. Rather, the 'cause' to my being 'here' is so infinitely more subtle and complex than I might like to assume that any attempts I might make to control or predict my future 'being here' experiences become singularly laughable.

The approach taken by existential psychotherapy may be rightfully considered as a sort of 'chaos theory of psychotherapy', for, like chaos theory proper, existential psychotherapy enjoins its practitioners to move on and away from their desires to predict and control their clients and, instead, urges them to approach matters from the standpoint of a new proposition – a proposition based, centrally, upon the acceptance of that mutual revelatory disclosure that is the expression of interrelational encounter. These chaos-acknowledging instances of the meeting of *self with other* seem to me to be not the predictable 'causes' for change, but rather serve as embodied confirmations of the actuality of being human and all the possibilities for freedom and responsibility therein contained and embraced. Such meetings, like that between a mirror and a hammer, may well be shattering. Yet, through their collision, the human truths that truly matter to us all, and that *are* our humanity, may stand revealed.

Throughout its first century, psychotherapy presented a version of itself that relied upon technological and utilitarian notions. *Here a mirror. There a hammer. Now, reflect. Now, smash. Now, rebuild. And, reflect once more.* This chapter, in common with the rest of this book, has sought to demonstrate the limits, and the limiting consequences, of this attitude, and I have suggested an alternative possibility. It is that which rests upon psychotherapy's exploration of those potentials which may arise when its practitioners come to acknowledge that, in their encounters with their clients, they are not the only ones who hold up mirrors and wield hammers.

Even more radically, through the implications of an interrelational focus upon meeting and encounter, a hint of something far more disturbing – and revealing – has begun to impose itself upon psychotherapeutic consciousness. This 'something' has neither yet been sufficiently acknowledged nor suitably identified other than by the tension-provoking label of 'chaos'. Perhaps, as I have sought to indicate, it is the task of existential psychotherapy to remind us that '*"Chaos" is the name we have given to an order that has not yet been understood*'.[25]

Notes

1 Celebrating mediocrity: what has happened to psychotherapy?

Some of the material covered in this chapter was first presented in various talks that I gave throughout 1999 and 2000. Some sections were previously published under the title 'If there are so many psychotherapies how come we keep making the same mistakes?', in *Psychotherapy in Australia*, 6(1): 16–22.

1. The quote by Murray Kempton appears in R. Baker, (1999) 'Decline and fall', *New York Review of Books*, XLVI (3) 4–6.
2. *The School of Psychotherapy and Counselling at Regent's College* has recently begun to offer intensive programmes focusing on mediation and alternative dispute resolution for lawyers and family mediators. Uniquely, the courses offer an approach that relies upon existential psychotherapy. A summary of its approach was prepared for the British Parliament's Hansard Society and was co-authored by Coleman, B., Coleman, S., Spinelli, E. and Strasser, F. (2000) 'Caught in the middle: training MP's in dispute resolution', in Power, G. (ed.) *Under Pressure: Are we Getting the Most from our MPs?*. London: Hansard Society Publications, pp. 37–44.
3. Sartre, J.-P. (1943) *Being and Nothingness*, trans. H. Barnes. New York: Philosophical Library (1956).
4. Coué, E. (1922) *Self-Mastery Through Auto Suggestion*. New York: Kessinger (1997). The original 'self-mastery' mantra is, of course, 'Every day, in every way, I get better and better'.
5. Mahrer, A. (1998) 'Embarrassing problems for the field of psychotherapy', *BPS Psychotherapy Section Newsletter*, 23: 3–25.
6. Nietzsche, F. (1961) *Thus Spoke Zarathustra*, trans. by R. J. Hollingdale. Harmondsworth: Penguin (1969).
7. Spinelli, E. (1994) *Demystifying Therapy*. London: Constable.
8. *Ibid*. The reference section of the text contains numerous sources dealing with psychotherapy research.

9. Excellent sources for further study of this point are: Roth, A. and Fonagy, P. (1996) *What Works For Whom: A Critical Review of Psychotherapy Research*. New York: Guilford; Miller, S. (2000) 'The myth of the magic pill', *Psychotherapy in Australia*, 6(3): 36–42; Pilgrim, D. (2000) 'More questions than answers', *The Psychologist*, 13(6): 302–5.

10. For good summary discussions of these views readers should turn to the relevant chapters in Woolfe, R. and Dryden, W. (eds) (1996) *Handbook of Counselling Psychology*. London: Sage.

11. The term 'existence tension' was coined by Bill Wahl (1999) (personal communication to author) who also kindly provided me with 'a preliminary list of those tensions which are intrinsic to human consciousness and existence'.

12. Spinelli, E. (1996) 'Existential-phenomenology for the consumer age: the promise and failure of *est*', *Journal of the Society for Existential Analysis*, 7(1): 2–25.

2 To disclose or to not disclose – that is the question

My 1994 Chair's Address to the Society for Existential Analysis forms an earlier version of this chapter. The talk was published under the title 'On disclosure', *Journal of the Society for Existential Analysis*, 6(1): 2–19.

1. For examples of Freud's fairly regular and consistent stretching and breaking of various fundamental 'rules' of psychoanalysis, see: Roazen, P. (1974) *Freud and His Followers*. Scarborough, Ontario: Meridian. (1976); Gay, P. (1988) *Freud: a Life for our Time*. London: J. M. Dent & Sons; Webster, R. (1995) *Why Freud Was Wrong: Sin, Science and Psychoanalysis*. London: HarperCollins.

2. For discussions on disclosure by psychoanalytic 'insiders' see: Fenichel, O. (1946) *The Psychoanalytic Theory of Neurosis*. London: Routledge & Kegan Paul (1982); Fine, R. (1979) *A History of Psychoanalysis*. Guildford, Surrey: Columbia University Press.

3. For a sound discussion of Robert Langs' derivative theory of communicative psychoanalysis, see Smith, D. L. (1991) *Hidden Conversations: An Introduction to Communicative Psychoanalysis*. London: Routledge.

4. Shaffer, J. B. P. (1978) *Humanistic Psychology*. London: Prentice-Hall.

5. Roeg, N. (director) (1973) *Don't Look Now*. London: British Lion Films.

6. Cf. Spinelli, *Demystifying Therapy.*
7. *Ibid.*
8. *Ibid.*

3 I am not a noun: the vagaries of the self

Some sections of this chapter appeared in a paper entitled 'The vagaries of the self', *Journal of the Society for Existential Analysis*, 7(2): 57–68.

1. See e.g. a fascinating discussion on Japanese views of the self in: Kondo, D. K. (1990) *Crafting Selves; Power, Gender, and Discourses of Identity in a Japanese Workplace.* London: University of Chicago Press. I also strongly recommend two brilliant books that touch on similar challenges to our notions of the self: Guidano, V. F. (1991) *The Self In Process: Toward a Post-rationalist Cognitive Therapy.* London: The Guilford Press; Harré, R. (1998) *The Singular Self: An Introduction to the Psychology of Personhood.* London: Sage.
2. Interesting versions of this argument can be found in: Gergen, K. J. (1991) *The Saturated Self: Dilemmas of Identity in Contemporary Life.* New York: Basic Books; Taylor, C. (1989) *Sources of the Self: The Making of the Modern Identity.* Cambridge: Cambridge University Press; Yardley, K. and Honess, T. (eds) (1987) *Self and Identity: Psychosocial Perspectives.* London: Wiley. The topic is also discussed regularly in the interdisciplinary *Journal of Consciousness Studies.*
3. For a detailed critique of these reductionist stances see Valle, R. S. and King, M. (1978) *Existential-Phenomenological Alternatives for Psychology.* New York: Oxford University Press.
4. A sound overview of narrative theory and psychotherapy appears in Freedman, J. and Combs, G. (1996) *Narrative Therapy: The Social Construction of Preferred Realities.* London: W. W. Norton.
5. See Ihde, D. (1986) *Experimental Phenomenology: An Introduction.* Albany: State University of New York Press; Spinelli, E. (1989) *The Interpreted World: An Introduction to Phenomenological Psychology.* London: Sage.
6. Cf. Ihde, *Experimental Phenomenology.*
7. *Ibid.*
8. Deurzen, E. van (1996) 'The survival of the self', *Journal of the Society for Existential Analysis*, 7(1): 56–66.
9. Heidegger, M. (1962) *Being And Time*, trans. by J. Macquarrie and E. Robinson. London: Harper & Row.

10. For those readers who do wish to examine and keep up with these debates, however, I can recommend no better source than the *Journal of Consciousness Studies*. For details and membership information contact the Journal at Imprint Academic, PO Box 1, Thorverton, EX5 5YX UK.
11. Cf. Deurzen, 'The survival of the self'.
12. *Ibid.*, p. 63.
13. *Ibid.*, p. 65.
14. Laing, R. D. (1959) *The Divided Self: An Existential Study in Sanity and Madness*. Harmondsworth: Penguin (1973).
15. Cooper, M. (1996) 'Modes of existence: towards a phenomenological polypsychism', *Journal of the Society for Existential Analysis*, 7(2): 50−6.
16. Vonnegut, K. (1968) *Mother Night*. London: Panther Books (1973). The complete and actual quote is as follows: This is the only story of mine whose moral I know. I don't think it's a marvellous moral; I simply happen to know what it is: We are what we pretend to be, so we must be careful about what we pretend to be. (p. vii).

4 Do we really need the unconscious?

1. Spinelli, E. (1993) 'The unconscious: an idea whose time has gone?', *Journal of the Society for Existential Analysis*, 4: 19−47; reprinted in Cohn, H. W. and Du Plock, S. (eds) (1995) *Existential Challenges to Psychotherapeutic Theory and Practice*, London: Existential Analysis Press, pp. 217−47.
2. Freud, S. (1916−17) 'Introductory lectures on psychoanalysis', in *Standard Edition*, vols 15 and 16, p. 278.
3. Erdelyi, M. H. (1985) *Psychoanalysis: Freud's Cognitive Psychology*. New York: W. H. Freeman. p. 61.
4. Smith, D. L. (1994) 'Riding shotgun for Freud: a reply to Ernesto Spinelli', *Journal of the Society for Existential Analysis*, 5: 145−6.
5. Freud, F. (1925) 'The resistances to psychoanalysis', in *Standard Edition*, Vol. 19, p. 31.
6. Gay, P. (1988) *Freud: A Life for our Time*. London: J. M. Dent & Sons. p. 128.
7. There exist so many excellent published views and debates on the question of consciousness that it is difficult to single out even a small number of texts. I suggest that interested readers pursue these debates

as they appear in the pages of the *Journal for Consciousness Studies* (see 3.9 above for further details).

8. Cf. Erdelyi, *Psychoanalysis.*
9. Whyte, L. L. (1978) *The Unconscious Before Freud.* London: Julian Friedmann, p. 63.
10. *Ibid.*, p. 21.
11. Cf. Erdelyi, *Psychoanalysis.*
12. Cf. Sartre, *Being and Nothingness.*
13. Cannon, B. (1991) *Sartre & Psychoanalysis: An Existentialist Challenge to Clinical Metatheory.* Lawrence: University Press of Kansas.
14. What is probably the most sustained critique of Sartre's argument appears in Gardner, S. (1993) *Irrationality and the Philosophy of Psychoanalysis.* Cambridge: Cambridge University Press.
15. Dixon, N. F. (1981) *Preconscious Processing.* New York: Wiley.
16. Sperry, R. W. (1970) 'Perception in the absence of neocortical commissures', in *Perception and Disorders* (Res. Publ. ARNMD, Vol. 48). New York: The Association for Research in Nervous and Mental Diseases.
17. See e.g. Edelman, G. (1992) *Bright Air, Brilliant Fire: On the Matter of the Mind.* Harmondsworth: Penguin (1994).
18. For discussions of this cf. Valle and King, *Existential-Phenomenological Alternatives for Psychology*; Spinelli, *The Interpreted World.*
19. Wittgenstein, L. (1982) 'Conversations on Freud: excerpt from 1932–3 lectures', in Wollheim, R. and Hopkins, J. (eds) *Philosophical Essays on Freud.* Cambridge: Cambridge University Press.
20. Cf. Erdelyi, *Psychoanalysis.*
21. *Ibid.* See also Webster, *Why Freud Was Wrong.*
22. Grotstein, J. S. (1992) 'Reflections on a century of Freud: some paths not chosen', *British Journal of Psychotherapy*, 9(2): 181–7.
23. Treisman, A. M. (1969) 'Strategies and models for selective attention', *Psychological Review*, 76: 282–99.
24. Cf. Dixon, *Preconscious Processing.*
25. Cf. Erdelyi, *Psychoanalysis.*
26. Miller, J. (1978) *The Body In Question.* London: Cape.
27. Sacks. O. (1985) *The Man Who Mistook His Wife For A Hat.* London: Duckworth.
28. Braude, S. E. (1991) *First Person Plural: Multiple Personality and the Philosophy of Mind.* London: Routledge.
29. Hacking, I. (1995) *Rewriting the Soul: Multiple Personality and the Sciences of Memory.* Chichester, NJ: Princeton University Press.

5 Reconfiguring human sexuality

My 1996 Chair's Address to the Society for Existential Analysis forms an earlier version of this chapter. The talk was published under the title 'Some hurried notes expressing outline ideas that someone might some-day utilise as signposts towards a sketch of an existential-phenomenological theory of human sexuality', *Journal of the Society for Existential Analysis*, 8(1): 2–20. A revised version of this talk was also published under the title 'Human sexuality: an existential-phenomenological inquiry', *Counselling Psychology Review*, 7(4): 170–8.

1. Heath, S. (1982) *The Sexual Fix*. London: Macmillan.
2. Foucault, M. (1979) *A History of Sexuality Vol 1: An Introduction*. London: Allen Lane; (1985) *A History of Sexuality Vol 2: The Use of Pleasure*. New York: Random House; (1986) *A History of Sexuality Vol 3: The Care of the Self*. New York: Random House.
3. Cf. Heath, *The Sexual Fix*, p. 21.
4. Dr Laws Milton's account and treatment for spermatorrhoea can be found in his 1887 pamphlet published under the title (but not under the counter) *The Pathology and Treatment of Spermatorrhoea*.
5. Sulloway, F. J. (1979) *Freud: Biologist of the Mind*. London: André Deutsch.
6. Merleau-Ponty, M. (1962) *Phenomenology of Perception*, trans. Colin Smith. London: Routledge & Kegan Paul.
7. Kovacs, G. (1993) 'The personalistic understanding of the body and sexuality in Merleau-Ponty', in Hoeller, K. (ed.) *Merleau-Ponty & Psychology*. Atlantic Highlands, NJ: Humanities Press, p. 210.
8. *Ibid.*, p. 211.
9. Cohn, H. W. (1997) *Existential Thought and Therapeutic Practice*. London: Sage.
10. Jordan, N. (director) (1992) *The Crying Game*. Film released by Palace Pictures.
11. Mahoney, E. R. (1983) *Human Sexuality*. London: McGraw-Hill.
12. Freud, E. (ed.) (1961) *Letters of Sigmund Freud 1873–1939*. London: Hogarth Press.
13. Dorner, G. (1976) *Hormones and Brain Differentiation*. Amsterdam: Elsevier.
14. Le Vay, S. (1996) *Queer Science*. Cambridge, MA: MIT Press.
15. Hamer, D. (1994) *The Science of Desire: The Search for the Gay Gene and the Biology of Behavior*. New York: Simon & Schuster.

16. Freud, S. (1956) 'Three essays on the theory of sexuality', in *Standard Edition*, Vol. 7.
17. *Ibid.*, p. 134.
18. Cf. Foucault, *A History of Sexuality Vol 1: An Introduction*, p. 43.
19. Kinsey, A. C., Pomeroy, W. B. and Martin, C. E. (1948) *Sexual Behavior in the Human Male*. Philadelphia, PA: W. B. Saunders.
20. Vidal, G. (1965) *The City & The Pillar*. London: John Lehmann Ltd.
21. Plummer, K. (1981) *The Making of the Modern Homosexual*. London: Hutchinson & Co.
22. Cf. Spinelli, *Demystifying Therapy*.
23. Cf. Sartre, *Being and Nothingness*.

6   Conflicting desires: childhood and sexuality

1. Cf. Sulloway, *Freud: Biologist of the Mind*.
2. *Ibid.*
3. Masson, J. M. (1984) *Freud: The Assault on Truth*. London: Faber and Faber.
4. Readers interested in the issues dealing with the history of the concept of childhood might refer to the following texts: Lascariges, C. and Hinitz, B. F. (2000) *History of Early Childhood Education*. New York: Falmer Press; Mussen, P. H., Conger, J. J. and Kagan, J. (1969) *Child Development and Personality*. New York: Harper & Row (later editions of this text unfortunately do not treat historical material quite so extensively as the first three editions).
5. Mussen, P. H., Conger, J. J., Kagan, J. and Huston, A. C. (1984) *Child Development and Personality*, 6th edn. London: Harper & Row.
6. Cf. Freud, *Standard Edition*, Vol. 7.
7. Klein, M. (1975) *The Psycho-Analysis of Children*. New York: Delta.
8. Jung, C. G. (1975) *Critique of Psychoanalysis*, trans. R. F. C. Hull. Princeton, NJ: Bollinger Series/Princeton University Press.
9. I am certain that, some years back, a book criticizing the impact of fashion-consciousness on children was published. I have tried to find a reference to this book, but so far have failed miserably. I am not even clear as to whether its author would agree with the views I am putting forward. However, if the missing source for the text finds its way to me, I will ensure that it is included in any later edition of this book that might be published.

7   **Psychotherapy and the challenge of evil**

This chapter is based upon the talk entitled 'Everything Is Broken' that I gave as my Inaugural Professorial Lecture in June, 1999. The talk was published in *The Psychotherapy Review*, 2(3). In addition, a summary paper entitled 'A personal view: therapy and the challenge of evil' appears in *British Journal of Guidance & Counselling*, 28(4): 561–7.

1. Arendt, H. (1973) *Origins of Totalitarianism*. New York: Harcourt Brace.
2. The quote by Hannah Arendt appears in Ignatieff, M. (1999) 'Human rights and the midlife crisis', *New York Review of Books*, 20 May, p. 59.
3. Steiner, G. (1983) *The Portage to San Cristobal of A.H.* New York: Washington Square Books.
4. Lang, B. (1996) *Heidegger's Silence*. Ithaca, NY: Cornell University Press.
5. The epistolary debate between Carl Rogers and Rollo May appears in Kirschenbaum, H. and Henderson, V. L. (eds) (1990) *Carl Rogers Dialogues*. London: Constable.
6. *Ibid.*
7. Ellenberger, H. F. (1970) *The Discovery of the Unconscious: The History and Evolution of Dynamic Psychiatry*. New York: Basic Books.
8. Rosenbaum, R. (1998) *Explaining Hitler: The Search for the Origins of his Evil*. London: Macmillan.
9. *Ibid.*
10. *Ibid.*, p. 86.
11. Milgram, S. (1974) *Obedience to Authority: An Experimental View*. New York: Harper & Row.
12. Zimbardo, P. G., Ebbesen, E. B. and Maslach, C. (1977) *Influencing Attitudes and Changing Behavior* (2nd edn). Reading, MA: Addison-Wesley.
13. Goldhagen, D. (1996) *Hitler's Willing Executioners*. New York: Pantheon.
14. Mantel, H. (1999) 'Killer children', *New York Review of Books*, 20 May, p. 6.
15. Arendt, H. (1994) *Eichmann in Jerusalem: A Report on the Banality of Evil* (revised edn). New York: Penguin, USA.
16. The quote by Primo Levi, taken from his book *Survival in Auschwitz* appears in Rosenbaum, *Explaining Hitler*, p. 275.

17. Peckinpah, S. (director) (1969) *The Wild Bunch*. Film released by Warner Brothers – Seven Arts.
18. Cf. Rosenbaum, *Explaining Hitler*.
19. Cooper, D. E. (1996) *Thinkers of Our Time – Heidegger*. London: Claridge Press.
20. Brooks, M. (1998) 'Quantum karma', *The Guardian Online Section*, 18 June, p. 13.
21. Nietzsche, F. (1879) *Human, All Too Human*, trans. R. J. Hollingdale. Cambridge: Cambridge University Press (1994).

8 Creation and being: a challenge to psychoanalytic theories of artistic creativity

My 1999 Chair's Address to the Society for Existential Analysis forms an earlier version of this chapter. The talk was published in 2000 under the title 'Creation and Being: existential-phenomenological challenges to psycho-analytic theories of artistic creativity', *Journal of the Society for Existential Analysis*, 11(1), pp. 2–20.

1. Winner, E. (1982) *Invented Worlds: The Psychology of the Arts*. London: Harvard University Press.
2. Arnheim, R. (1972) *Toward a Psychology of Art*. Berkeley, CA: University of California Press.
3. Cf. Winner, *Invented Worlds*.
4. Freud, S. (1958) *On Creativity and the Unconscious*. New York: Harper & Row.
5. Fuller, P. (1990) *Art and Psychoanalysis*. London: Artists and Readers.
6. Cf. Freud, *On Creativity and the Unconscious*.
7. Grünbaum, A. (1984) *The Foundations of Psychoanalysis: A Philosophical Critique*. London: University of California Press.
8. Storr, A. (1972) *The Dynamics of Creation*. London: Secker & Warburg.
9. *Ibid*.
10. Cf. Freud, *On Creativity and the Unconscious*, pp. 44–54.
11. Kris, E. (1952) *Psychoanalytic Explorations in Art*. New York: International Universities Press.
12. Cf. Storr, *The Dynamics of Creation*.
13. *Ibid*.
14. *Ibid*.
15. Delbanco, A. (1999) 'The decline and fall of literature', *The New York Review of Books*, 56(17): 32–8.

16. Goguen, J. A. (2000) 'What is art?', *Journal of Consciousness Studies*, 7(8–9): 7–15.
17. Heidegger, M. (1960) *Poetry, Language, Thought*, trans. A. Hofstadeter. London: Harper & Row (1975).
18. Heidegger, M. (1971) *On The Way to Language*, trans. A. Hofstadeter. London: Harper & Row.
19. Thompson, M. G. (1997) 'Logos, poetry and Heidegger's conception of creativity', *Psychotherapy in Australia*, 3(4): 60–5.
20. Cf. Goguen, 'What is art?', p. 10.
21. Cf. Fuller, *Art and Psychoanalysis*.
22. Kockelmans, J. (1985) *Heidegger on Art and Art Work*. Dordrecht: Martinus Nijhoff.
23. May, R. (1975) *The Courage To Create*. New York: W. W. Norton.
24. *Ibid.*
25. Scarry, E. (1999) *On Beauty and Being Just*. Princeton, NJ: Princeton University Press.
26. The quote by Elaine Scarry appears in Hampshire, S. (1999) 'The eye of the beholder', *New York Review of Books*, 56(18): 42.
27. *Ibid.*
28. Steiner, G. (1989) *Real Presences*. Chicago, IL: University of Chicago Press.
29. The quote by George Steiner appears in Fuller, P. (1990) *Images of God*. London: Writers and Readers. p. 23.
30. Cf. Hampshire, 'The eye of the beholder', p. 44.
31. Allen, W. (director) (1979) *Manhattan*. Film released by United Artists.

9   Beyond the great beyond

My 1998 Chair's Address to the Society for Existential Analysis forms an earlier version of this chapter. The talk was published in 1998 under the title 'Existential encounters with the paranormal and the uncanny', *Journal of the Society for Existential Analysis*, 9(2): 2–17.

1. Freud, S. (1963) *Studies in Parapsychology*. New York: Collier.
2. Jung, C. G. (1973) *Synchronicity: An Acausal Connecting Principle*. Princeton, NJ: Bollinger Series/Princeton University Press.
3. Whitehouse, T. (1999) 'Therapists' views of transpersonal communication within psychotherapy', *British Psychological Society Abstracts of the BPS Transpersonal Psychology Section 1999 Annual Conference*, p. 12.

4. Spinelli, E. (1978) *Human Development and Paranormal Cognition.* unpublished Ph.D. Thesis, University of Surrey, UK.

5. *Ibid.*

6. Cf. Ihde, *Experimental Phenomenology*; Spinelli, *The Interpreted World.*

7. Strawson, G. (1997) 'The self', *Journal of Consciousness Studies*, 4(5/6): 405–28.

8. Spinelli, E. (1997) *Tales of Un-knowing: Therapeutic Encounters from an Existential Perspective.* London: Duckworth.

9. Stern, D. (1985) *The Interpersonal World of the Infant: A View from Psychoanalysis and Developmental Psychology.* New York: Basic Books.

10. Kegan, R. (1982) *The Evolving Self: Problem and Process in Human Development.* London: Harvard University Press.

11. Ehrenwald, J. (1971) 'Mother–child symbiosis: the cradle of ESP', *Psychoanalytic Review*, 58: 455–66.

12. Carington, W. (1949) *Matter, Mind and Meaning.* London: Methuen.

13. Cf. Spinelli, *The Interpreted World.*

14. Wolman, B. J. (ed.) (1977) *Handbook of Parapsychology.* London: Van Nostrand Reinhold.

15. May, R. (1969) *Love and Will.* New York: Delta.

16. Koestler, A. (1982) 'Suicide note'. Copies of this document were included in a memorial pamphlet made available to those who attended a meeting to honour the memory of Arthur Koestler and Cynthia Koestler, held at The Royal Academy of Arts, London, UK on Thursday, 7 April 1983.

17. Cf. Sartre, *Being and Nothingness.*

10 The mirror and the hammer: some hesitant steps towards a more humane psychotherapy

1. See e.g. Masson, J. (1989) *Against Therapy.* London: Collins; Russell J. (1993) *Out of Bounds.* London: Sage; Smail, D. (1996) *How To Survive Without Psychotherapy.* London: Constable; Lomas, P. (1999) *Doing Good? Psychotherapy out of its Depth.* Oxford: Oxford University Press.

2. Sands, A. (2000) *Falling for Therapy: Psychotherapy From a Client's Point of View.* London: Macmillan.

3. Gordon, E. F. (2000) *Mockingbird Years: A Life In and Out of Therapy.* New York: Basic Books.

4. Spinelli, E. (1995) 'Afterword', in Alexander, R. *Folie a Deux: An Experience of One-to-one Therapy*. London: Free Association Books.
5. Cf. Gordon, *Mockingbird Years*, p. 16.
6. *Ibid.* p. 16.
7. *Ibid.* p. 119.
8. *Ibid.* p. 125.
9. *Ibid.* p. 126.
10. *Ibid.* p. 218.
11. *Ibid.* p. 221.
12. Farber, L. H. (1967) 'Martin Buber and psychotherapy', in Schilpp, P. A. and Friedman, M. (eds) *The Philosophy of Martin Buber*. The Library of Living Philosophers, vol. XII. La Salle, IL: Open Court. (A collection of Leslie Farber's most important papers under the title *The Ways of Will* was published in December 2000 by New York: Basic Books.)
13. *Ibid.*, p. 578.
14. *Ibid.*, p. 590.
15. *Ibid.*, p. 594.
16. *Ibid.*, p. 596.
17. *Ibid.*, p. 596.
18. Various references to Martin Buber's *Between Man and Man* and *I and Thou* appear throughout Farber's paper (*ibid*).
19. Cf. Gordon, *Mockingbird Years*, p. 224.
20. *Ibid.*, p. 225.
21. *Ibid.*, p. 126.
22. Kierkegaard, S. (1960) *The Diary of Søren Kierkegaard*, ed. Peter Rohde. New York: Philosophical Library (1990).
23. Cf. Gordon, *Mockingbird Years*, p. 228–9.
24. Gleick, J. (1988) *Chaos: Making a New Science*. London: Cardinal.
25. Miller, H. (1961) *Tropic of Capricorn*. New York: Grove Press. The actual quote is as follows: 'Confusion is a word we have invented for an order which is not understood.' My hope is that Mr Miller is too busy up in heaven teaching angels all there is to know about sex for him to be much bothered by my paraphrasing of this great sentence.